FREUD AND RELIGIOUS BELIEF

FREUD
AND
RELIGIOUS
BELIEF

by

H. L. Philp
Ph.D.

ROCKLIFF

SALISBURY SQUARE · LONDON

1956

Printed in Great Britain by
The Camelot Press Ltd., London and Southampton

FOR

E. A. B.

Acknowledgments

I WISH to thank the following publishers for their kindness in granting me permission to use extracts from their publications:

KEGAN PAUL   B. Malinowski, *Sex and Repression in Savage Society* (1927)

HARCOURT, BRACE & CO., NEW YORK   A. L. Kroeber, *Anthropology* (1948)

ALLEN & UNWIN   Edited by Sandor Lorand, *Psycho-analysis Today* (1948)

ANGUS & ROBERTSON, SYDNEY   A. P. Elkin, *The Australian Aborigines* (1938)

COHEN & WEST   A. R. Radcliffe-Brown, *Structure and Function in Primitive Society* (1952)

ROUTLEDGE & KEGAN PAUL   R. Firth, *Primitive Economics of the New Zealand Maori* (1929)

DUCKWORTH & CO.   J. C. Flugel, *Man, Morals and Society* (1945)

THE JOHNS HOPKINS PRESS, BALTIMORE   W. F. Albright, *From the Stone Age to Christianity* (1946)

CHARLES SCRIBNER'S SONS   J. H. Breasted, *The Dawn of Conscience* (1934)

PENGUIN BOOKS   H. & H. A. Frankfort, J. A. Wilson, T. Jacobsen, *Before Philosophy* (1949)

HARPER & BROTHERS, NEW YORK   T. J. Meek, *Hebrew Origins* (1950)

HOGARTH PRESS   Ernest Jones, *Sigmund Freud—Life and Work*, vol. I (1953)

Sigmund Freud, trans. James Strachey, *An Autobiographical Study* (1935)

Sigmund Freud, *Collected Papers*, vol. II (1924)

Sigmund Freud, trans. W. D. Robson-Scott, *The Future of an Illusion* (1949)

Sigmund Freud, trans. K. Jones, *Moses and Monotheism* (1939)

Sigmund Freud, trans. W. J. H. Sprott (2nd edn.), *New Introductory Lectures on Psycho-Analysis* (1937)

T. Reik, *From Thirty Years with Freud* (1942)

Preface

SIGMUND FREUD was possibly the greatest psychologist the world has ever known. The term 'unconscious' was, of course, known long before his time, but merely as a remote concept. It was Freud who discovered the living reality, and, what is even more significant, began its exploration through psychoanalysis. It was he who initiated the scientific study of dreams, another insight of genius which, after years of patient work, he gave to the world in *The Interpretation of Dreams*. Freud in fact added another dimension to men's thinking and experience.

Some people have moral and others physical courage, but Freud was among those who possessed both. We see his moral courage in the fearlessness with which he gave his message during the first lonely years when the world, including even his medical colleagues, listened in silence—or not at all. How revealing was his reaction when he heard Charcot privately admit the relation of sexual factors to certain nervous symptoms and say, " 'Mais, dans ces pareils c'est toujours la chose genitale, toujours—toujours—toujours.' I know that for one second I was almost paralysed with amazement and said to myself, 'Well, but if he knows that, why does he never say so?' "* Freud had the moral courage to follow what he believed to be the truth wherever it might lead. For the last sixteen years of his life he suffered from a painful cancer in the mouth which he bore stoically, continuing his work almost without interruption.

His integrity was related to the quality of his courage for he not only hated hypocrisy and pretence, but fought it wherever he found it. Illustrating this is Reik's description of the occasion on which he gave the funeral address for his distinguished friend, Karl Abraham, at a meeting of the Vienna Psychoanalytical Society. Freud was present at the meeting, although

* *Collected Papers*, vol. 1, p. 295.

too ill to give the address, and "on the way home he com-
mended me for mentioning not only the virtues of our friend,
but his faults also. 'That is just the way I should have done it,
Reik', he said. 'The proverb, *de mortuis nil nisi bonum*, is, I think,
nothing but a relic of our primitive fear of the dead. We psychoanalysts must throw such conventions overboard. Trust the
others to remain hypocrites even before the coffin.' "* This is
the real Freud, superior perhaps but not lacking in integrity,
and if there is a hardness in his virtue it reminds us that he too
is human.

Those who have disliked his theories have often sought to
disparage their creator, and some readers may hope to find in
this book an attempt to lower the stature of a great man; if so
they will be disappointed. In a Preface one can be personal,
and I should like therefore to express my warm admiration both
for his pioneer work and for the man himself.

Admiration of Freud, however, need not be blind adulation,
nor imply a belief that all his work is of equal value. Freud
praised Reik for mentioning the faults as well as the virtues of
Abraham, and our honesty must be no less. His claim to fame is as
a psychologist, and he had no special qualifications in other
subjects such as anthropology, history or theology. Yet we find
him making definite pronouncements on historical problems
including, for example, the astounding claim that there was a
second Moses. There were, too, forays into theology, and
God was abased to an 'exalted Father' figure and original sin
explained as racial guilt caused by the slaying of the father of
the horde.

Yet even here Freud's integrity is not in question, and certainly
not his courage. Convinced that he was right in his atheism, he
naturally concluded that religion was an obstinate illusion, a
mass neurosis, and he never doubted that it could be explained
away. His own courage needed no illusions to sustain it; the universe might be barren and ultimately without purpose but he
would face it unafraid. Suspicious of wishes promising hope and

* *From Thirty Years with Freud*, by Theodor Reik (1942), pp. 15-16.

happiness, he was determined not to be deceived, and his view of reality was so fixed that everything he perceived was determined by it. Inevitably his microscopic gaze in a particular direction excluded large parts of the universe.

Consciously Freud treated religion as an illusion, but paid it so much attention that one suspects it was unconsciously more important than he realized. It is significant that in one of his later essays, "A Philosophy of Life,"* he gives approximately two-thirds of the space to a consideration of religion, which thus proves itself to be a remarkably vigorous illusion.

I believe that Freud's case against religion in general was unsound, and reflected his own opinions rather than the findings of psychoanalysis. It is noteworthy that his chief works on religious subjects such as *Totem and Taboo*, *The Future of an Illusion* and *Moses and Monotheism* are the most neglected of his books to-day. Specialists in the subjects around which Freud's arguments in these books are built, reject his findings with remarkable unanimity. Their certainty indeed leads them to assume that Freud's writings on these subjects must belong to the dead past, and that it is no longer worth while answering his contentions. This attitude overlooks the fact that Freud's personal convictions about religion, which are well known, are given by many an undue importance because of his immense fame and the dynamic influence of psychoanalysis. Many of those who have never studied his writings on religion assume, or half-assume, that religion must be false because Freud said so.

For over twenty years I have had an intense interest in Freudian theories. As a university lecturer on social psychology I have emphasized their importance, and this book has grown out of a lecture I first gave to a university society. One difficulty I have had in writing it is that in studying Freud's work I have come to realize that no one man can be a specialist in general and social psychology, psychiatry, theology, Old Testament criticism, Egyptology, pre-history, anthropology and philosophy. Yet on most of these subjects Freud confidently made pronouncements.

* *New Introductory Lectures on Psychoanalysis* (1933).

As it happens my studies and interests have been concerned with a number of these subjects, but on all of them I have sought and obtained guidance from experts to whom I am grateful, although I alone am responsible for what has been written.

Freud's views on religion are widely scattered in his writings, and I could not assume that all my readers would be acquainted with everything that he wrote. It has been necessary, therefore, to outline his main themes and at times to quote extensively in the interests of intelligibility and fairness.

I have been greatly helped in my understanding of Freud's early years by Dr. Ernest Jones's *Sigmund Freud*, Vol. I, a finely written and convincing study. Unfortunately Dr. Jones has not yet published Vol. III but he has been kind enough to discuss with me such theories as the primal horde, original sin, the racial unconscious, the possibility of an Egyptian Moses and a second Moses. I owe much to this, although I ventured to differ from Dr. Jones on most of the subjects. We are, however, in complete agreement in our admiration of Freud the man, and here Dr. Jones, who must know more about him than any other person, made what I had always felt to be the heroic stature of Freud himself, more real. Dr. Jones has added to his kindness by reading Chapter I, and although I have profited greatly by his suggestions, I must accept full responsibility for all that is included.

I should like to express my sincere gratitude to Dr. E. A. Bennet, consulting psychiatrist, and also to my former colleague, Dr. M. Hewitt, Lecturer in Sociology in the University of Exeter, both of whom have read the whole of my manuscript and made valuable criticisms, emendations and suggestions. I am also grateful to Dr. J. B. Loudon, who, as an anthropologist, helped to guide my reading for the chapter on Totem and Taboo and added to his kindness by reading it. The Revd. U. E. Simon, Lecturer in Old Testament Exegesis and Hebrew at King's College in the University of London, gave me valuable help by reading the chapter on Moses and Monotheism. My former research student, Dr. G. B. Trasler, has checked the references throughout with the thoroughness which has distinguished his research work. Miss M. K. Tyler has been responsible for all the typing during the preparation of the manuscript and I owe much to her patient and efficient work.

Contents

1

An Unrepentant Atheist

"He grew up devoid of any belief in a God or Immortality and does not appear to have felt the need of it."

"... he was always an unrepentant atheist."
ERNEST JONES, *Sigmund Freud* (vol. I, pp. 22 and 33).

"Even when I have moved away from observation, I have carefully avoided any contact with philosophy proper. This avoidance has been greatly facilitated by constitutional incapacity."
SIGMUND FREUD, *An Autobiographical Study* (p. 109).

I

FREUD was an atheist from such an early age that speculation immediately arises about the experiences and facts which led him to take up so definite a position. In obedience to his own teaching, we must attempt to evaluate the effect of those who surrounded him during his earliest years: father, mother, brothers and sisters, nurse and also other children. There, as he would have said, we have the chief sources of what a man becomes: his personality, his neuroses and his beliefs. What, then, do we know of Freud's infancy, of his parents, and of all the other influences which, if he had been analysing a patient, he would have concluded had at least helped to determine his beliefs about religion? We must consider too the impact of the general atmosphere of his education, the predominating scientific and philosophical tendencies of the period, and the fact that he was born into an unpopular minority, the Jews.

Whatever the force of all these factors may have been, there is no doubt about the truth of the statement by Dr. Ernest Jones in his *Sigmund Freud:* "He [Freud] grew up devoid of any belief

I

in a God or Immortality, and does not appear to have felt the need of it. The emotional needs that usually manifest themselves in adolescence found expression, first in rather vague philosophical cogitations, and, soon after, in an earnest adherence to the principles of science."[1]

Freud belonged to a middle-class Jewish family; his great-grandfather was called Rabbi Ephraim Freud, and his grandfather, from whom he received his Jewish name, was Rabbi Schlome Freud. The title Rabbi is not necessarily an ecclesiastical one but was frequently used as a polite gesture.

His father, Jakob Freud, who was born in Galicia, was a merchant dealing principally in wool. He was not very successful in his business ventures and Freud described him as "always hopefully expecting something to turn up". Jakob Freud was of a gentle disposition, with a sense of humour, and his family had a real affection for him. Undoubtedly his liberalism and free-thinking had their influence on Freud himself.

Freud's mother was Jakob Freud's second wife and was under twenty when Jakob, aged forty, married her. She outlived her husband by thirty-four years and reached the age of ninety-five. As a young woman she was slender and pretty and, to the end of her life, gay, alert and quick-witted. By his first wife, Jakob had had two sons. Sigmund was the eldest child of the second family and subsequently there were five daughters and two more sons. Freud always felt that as the first-born he was his mother's favourite child and in fact he wrote later: "A man who has been the indisputable favourite of his mother keeps for life the feeling of a conqueror, that confidence of success that often induces real success."[2] He retained a feeling of confidence and attributed it to the sense of security given him by his mother's love.

There is some uncertainty about the exact nature of Freud's religious background. His father was brought up as an orthodox Jew, and Freud was familiar with Jewish customs and festivals. Sigmund Freud's children assured Ernest Jones that Jakob "had become a complete free-thinker". Dr. Jones thinks that there is evidence which suggests otherwise, but it is difficult to see how the family could have gained this impression without good reasons. If Jakob had remained an orthodox Jew surely his grandchildren, who were vitally interested in this subject because of their father's views, must have been aware of the fact. He was, in any case, looked upon as a liberal-minded man with progressive views, and it is certain that he did not continue the orthodox customs after moving to Vienna when Freud was just four years old. All the indications, therefore, are that Freud was brought up in a family where the old religious traditions and customs were steadily dying out.

On the other side, Freud's son Ernst possesses a Bible which Jakob, then seventy-five years old, presented to Sigmund on his thirty-fifth birthday. The incription, in Hebrew, reads:

My dear Son

It was in the seventh year of your age that the spirit of God began to move you to learning. I would say the spirit of God speaketh to you: "Read in My book; there will be opened to thee sources of knowledge of the intellect." It is the Book of Books; it is the well that wise men have digged and from which lawgivers have drawn the waters of their knowledge. Thou hast seen in this Book the vision of the Almighty, thou hast heard willingly, thou hast done and hast tried to fly high upon the wings of the Holy Spirit. Since then I have preserved the same Bible. Now, on your thirty-fifth birthday I have brought it out from its retirement and I send it to you as a token of love from your old father.

The precise significance of this inscription is difficult to interpret. It is, in any case, a formal, indefinite statement. It was certainly not true that Freud had seen in this book the vision of the Almighty. Freud had made up his mind long before he was thirty-five that there was no Almighty. Perhaps the key to the gift lies in the words "I have brought it out from its retirement and I send it to you as a token of love from your old father".

B

From all that we can gather the Old Testament, and with it the Jewish customs and ceremonies, had probably been in retirement for a long time, but there was a stirring in the aged Jakob when his son was thirty-five and he an old man of seventy-five. He was still a Jew and the Old Testament was the Book, the literature of his race, and this a family Bible, and so he passed it over, as a Jewish father would. The most significant factor in the gift was probably that it was a token of love.

Freud later spoke of having been greatly influenced by his early reading of the Bible but, according to Dr. Ernest Jones, " . . . he can only have meant in an ethical sense, in addition to his historical interest".[3]

We know very little of the religious outlook of Freud's mother. But we do know that she wrote him a letter in 1886, when, as a married man, he was going to set up in practice, and in this earnestly asked for the blessing of Almighty God on his endeavours, although this may have been no more than a pious phrase.

There was, however, one very definite religious influence in Freud's earliest years for in their household there was a Catholic nurse, although this particular influence was not one that predisposed Freud towards religion. This nurse was old and ugly and although she undoubtedly possessed affection for the children she could also be severe. At the same time she was capable and efficient. Freud referred to her in his writings a number of times as "that prehistoric old woman". Yet he was fond of her and curiously enough gave her his pocket money. She was a Czech and they talked in that language although Freud forgot it later. What was perhaps important was that she took Freud with her to church services and gave him ideas about heaven and hell, and almost certainly about other Christian teachings. The child was obviously impressed because he reports that when they returned from church he used to preach a sermon and expound God's doings. Unfortunately, when Sigmund was two and a half years old, the nurse was dismissed for theft. It is difficult at this distance to obtain all the facts that one would like and so estimate correctly

the influence of this important figure during the very impressionable years of Freud's life, but Dr. Jones comments ". . . perhaps
her terrifying influence contributed to his later dislike of Christian
beliefs and ceremonies."[4] Clearly she was the figure in his early
days who was associated with religion and especially with the
Christian religion. But, unfortunately, she was found to be a
thief. Although the Freud family at that time were not practising
members of the Jewish community, they no doubt retained the
strict moralistic outlook of their traditional religion, and the
commandment from the Decalogue "Thou shalt not steal"
would be important to them. In Freud's later theories the significance of the father and mother and other figures in the family
circle during the earliest years of life is stressed. An intelligent
child senses the attitude of his family towards any member of the
household, and it is difficult not to believe that although Freud
was not told about the thefts until he was nearly grown up, he
knew that the nanny of whom he had been fond was no longer
trusted and respected. In fact any mystery about her departure
might make her all the more a dark figure. On an impressionable
child the whole episode would have a profound effect and,
what is more important, this would be largely unconscious.
Even when as a young man he learnt the facts about why she
had suddenly disappeared he probably felt that she was a fraud,
and with his background this was not likely to make him more
favourably disposed towards religion.

But it was not one experience alone which gave Freud his
strong bias against religion; one traumatic experience cannot
determine the whole future. The general influence of the whole
environment is far more important, and it must be remembered
that Freud's father did become something of a free-thinker.
The whole religious structure must have been weakening in the
family or the child would never have been allowed to attend a
Catholic church, and all that Freud did was to carry on the
movement to what appeared to him to be its logical conclusion.
That is to say the family gave up Jewish ceremonies and customs
and, of course, the beliefs which lay behind them. With his

family background it only needed an experience such as that of the dishonest Catholic nurse to cause a complete break with any slight religious outlook he may have found in his home, and change him into a convinced atheist. At any rate there is no doubt that this is what he did become.

II

His birthplace, Freiberg, was a town of about 5,000 inhabitants, almost all of whom were Roman Catholics. The small non-conforming section was composed of two per cent. Protestant and the same percentage of Jews. The town itself was dominated by a 200-foot steeple which possessed the finest chimes in the province. Freud must have come to realize as he was taken to this church by his nurse that his family belonged to a minority and, as Ernest Jones says, "the chimes rang out not brotherly love but hostility to the little circle of non-believers. Perhaps there was an echo of these chimes in the night long after when his sleep was disturbed by church bells so that, to put an end to the annoyance, he dreamed that the Pope was dead."[5] The dream was true but not perhaps in the way that Freud interpreted it, for we are seldom the truest interpreters of our own dreams. Religion, symbolized by the bells, continued to disturb him, as his writings reveal, but for him the Pope had died long ago—perhaps when his nurse had been caught stealing.

His early years were a time of great anxiety and hardship as far as his family was concerned. Jakob Freud carried on his business as a wool merchant at Freiberg but, unfortunately, for about twenty years before Sigmund was born, textile manufacturing on which the town depended had been failing. The increasing use of machines had here, as elsewhere, led to unemployment among the hand-workers. Another blow to the town was struck when the new Northern Railway from Vienna by-passed it and took trade elsewhere. After the Restoration of 1851 there was inflation which led to still more poverty, and when the Austro-Italian war came in 1859 Freiberg was a distressed, disheartened and poverty-stricken town.

Naturally, Jakob's business shared in these misfortunes. In addition, Czech nationalism became a powerful force after the 1848-49 revolution. Inevitably, therefore, the Czechs opposed the German-Austrians who were the ruling class in Bohemia and Moravia and, as the Jews were German-speaking as well as being traditional scapegoats, the hatred was soon directed against them. In Prague itself the revolution had begun with riots against the Jewish textile manufacturers. In Freiberg, where the cloth-makers were all Czechs, the Jewish woollen merchants were inevitably held responsible. They felt in some danger of attack and, in any case, had little possibility of earning a livelihood. When Freud was three years old the family moved to Leipsic and then, a year later, to Vienna.

By this time Freud had a background of grinding poverty and it is small wonder that he came to hate it so much. He knew it as a boy and as a student; it prevented him for a long time from marrying, and even as late as May 1885, the year before his marriage, he wrote: "The same yearly and daily questions, no money at home, no fire in the stove, mother ill and in need of country air."[6] The year before there had been a review of the hopeless financial situation in his home and various members of the family undertook different responsibilities. Freud's share was ten gulden a month. In addition he provided ten gulden a month for his brother's training. There was a continuing struggle with poverty for years after his marriage; in fact it was surprisingly late in life, considering his immense fame, that his financial circumstances became easier.

III

As an infant Freud was taught first by his mother, and then by his father. Later he was sent to a private school and at nine he passed the entrance examination to the Sperl Gymnasium. Here he revealed both his intelligence and his industry for, spending eight years there, he was at the top of the class for seven of them. In his *An Autobiographical Study* he mentions that he enjoyed special privileges and "was required to pass scarcely any examinations".[7] He was placed in the standard *summa cum laude*. As a reward for his achievements his father promised him a visit to England which took place two years after he left.

By the time he was ready to go on to a university he knew his real interests. He had "a sort of curiosity, which was, however, directed more towards human concerns than towards natural objects".[8] He mentions too that in later life he recognized that his early familiarity with the Bible story had "an enduring effect upon the direction of my interest". Other influences were important too. One of the chief of these was the theories of Darwin, then at the height of their impact, which he found very attractive, especially as "they held out hopes of an extraordinary advance in our understanding of the world . . ."[9] In the same sentence he wrote that "it was hearing Goethe's beautiful essay on Nature read aloud at a popular lecture by Professor Carl Brühl" just before he left school which made him decide to become a medical student.

Freud's reactions to this pantheistic essay of Goethe's, glorifying Nature as a bountiful mother loving her children, are complex. Like Goethe, he had been attracted by the study of law. Goethe, however, turned to the natural sciences but his final and lasting concern was for imaginative literature, and he is outstanding for the range of his interests and speculations, and the breadth and depth of his personal experience.

Wittels, in his *Sigmund Freud* (1924) asserts that Freud told Stekel that he had once thought of becoming a novelist so that he could pass on to posterity what he had learnt from his patients. This reveals interests far wider than the strict path of science which was his first choice. Natural science may be chosen as a study because of one's interest in natural phenomena, but as Wittels concludes: "On the other hand, he may be one whose bent towards abstractions is so powerful that he is afraid of being mastered by it, and feels it necessary to study concrete science as a counterpoise. Certainly that is how it was with me. I became a medical student in order to keep my feet firmly planted on the solid ground of fact. I fancy Freud may have been influenced by similar motives. He studied assiduously and perseveringly in the school of facts."[10]

Possibly Wittels is correct in his suggested diagnosis: at least, Freud did not make a special point of contradicting it in the letter he wrote to Wittels after reading the book. What is more certain is that he was not so wholly absorbed in scientific questions as he had once thought himself to be. In the Postscript he wrote to *An Autobiographical Study* in 1935 he said: "My interest, after making a lifelong *détour* through the natural sciences, medicine and psychotherapy, returned to the cultural problems which had fascinated me long before, when I was a youth scarcely old enough for thinking."[11]

Yet his views about the cultural problems which could profitably be investigated were very rigid, and religious interpretations of them were completely ruled out. Dr. Jones, commenting on the influence of Goethe, said: "There is no reason to think that Freud ever cudgelled his brains about the purpose of the Universe—he was always an unrepentant atheist—but that mankind was moved by various purposes, motives, aims, many of which need not be evident ones, was a conception he must always have had in his mind, long before he developed it so brilliantly by solving the riddle of the Sphinx."[12]

When he was forty, Freud said, in a letter to Fliess, that as a young man he longed for nothing but philosophical knowledge, and that at the time of writing he was on the way to satisfying this longing by turning over from medicine to psychology.

In 1873 he joined the University of Vienna as a medical student. He had to earn a living and as a Jew the opportunities of doing this were limited: medicine was one of the most promising ways. He realized too that although his speculative interests were very extensive a limit must be set to them. So much was unknowable and he wanted to study what could be known; as for the rest he was agnostic and in religion atheistic. He was very receptive to the scientific atmosphere then prevailing in the medical schools of Austria and Germany.

Convinced as he was of the immense possibilities for the understanding of the world provided by Darwin's theories, Freud threw himself into his scientific studies with all the tremendous concentration and industry of which he was capable. If science held the key to the future which was full of unlimited possibilities for progress, then it was essential that he should qualify himself as a scientist with complete self-discipline.

Thus he entered Vienna University eager for a scientific training, and he found that which he sought in Brücke's physiological laboratory. Brücke, who was Professor of Physiology in Vienna from 1849 to 1890, was a brilliant scientist. Moreover, he was in close touch with the outstanding scientific men of his age and so with all the latest developments. He was a prominent member of an influential scientific movement led by Helmholtz, whose name is always associated with the formulation of the law of the conservation of energy, and whose work in physiology and psychology was of lasting importance. The views of the Helmholtz school on the nervous system dominated German physiologists and medical teachers. Although their influence had probably passed its greatest period by the time Freud became a student, it was still important in the teaching of physiology. Later, when Helmholtz visited Vienna, Freud regretted missing him and wrote: "He is one of my idols."[13] Helmholtz and Brücke, together with Emil Du Bois-Reymond and Carl Ludwig, formed a private club in the early 'forties and became the spearhead of the movement. Brücke was indeed called "our ambassador in the Far East"—the Far East being Vienna. The spirit of the movement is shown by what Du Bois-Reymond wrote in 1842: "Brücke and I pledged a solemn oath to put into effect this truth: 'No other forces than the common physical and chemical ones are active within the organism. In those cases which cannot at the time be explained by these forces one has either to find the specific way or form of their action by means of the physical-mathematical method or to assume new forces equal in dignity to the chemical-physical forces inherent in matter, reducible to the force of attraction and repulsion.' "[14]

At this stage in his life it was natural that Freud made Brücke his master and hero. For above everything else Brücke was the type of disciplined scientist that Freud aspired to be. Brücke, who was a German, placed great emphasis on the thorough use of scientific method based on painstaking observation and description. Freud realized how much he owed to Brücke, and in his *An Autobiographical Study* he acknowledged his obligation: "At length, in Ernst Brücke's physiological laboratory, I found rest and satisfaction—and men, too, whom I could respect and take as my models: the great Brücke himself, and his assistants Sigmund Exner and Ernst von Fleischl-Marxow."[15] In fact he found so much rest and satisfaction there and pursued his research to such an extent that he did not take his degree of Doctor of Medicine until he had been a student for eight years instead of the usual five.

Brücke published his Lectures in Physiology in 1874 and Freud also found great satisfaction in them. It was a physiology influenced by the principle of the conservation of energy, with an emphasis on the dynamic character of the forces involved, and evolutionary concepts were prominent in it. Thus Freud found in the man himself, in his methods and in his teaching, all that he sought. Later he said that he considered Brücke the greatest authority he had ever met. For the next ten years at least the spirit of Brücke continued to dominate him, and the image of those steel-grey eyes as a symbol of the spirit of dedicated scientific research remained with him for the rest of his life.

IV

It must not be thought, however, that other currents did not reach Freud, and one of them was *Naturphilosophie*. This system, which owed much to the philosopher Schelling, was an attempt to find unity and spiritual meaning in all the events of the natural order. Schelling thought that nature and spirit were complementary parts of one whole. In practice, however, *Naturphilosophie* became a popular movement of a rather mystical nature in opposition to the analytical tendency of the eighteenth century. Goethe, whom Freud admired, had been an early supporter of *Naturphilosophie* and, for a brief space, Freud caught the enthusiasm.

But this phase soon passed and Freud returned to the spirit and methods of his master, Brücke. In Brücke's laboratory he worked resolutely at the problems which were given him. They were very appropriate for the time and place but they were remote in spirit and material from the problems discussed in *Totem and Taboo, Moses and Monotheism* and *Civilization and its Discontents*, and even for what we should now call orthodox psychoanalysis. Freud's first work in Brücke's laboratory was a microscopic investigation of the histology of the nerve cells, and this was of sufficient merit to secure the appreciation of his exacting professor. Brücke was interested in the histology of the cells of the spinal cord, and Freud's next research was on the spinal cord of one of the lowest of the fishes (*Ammocoetes Petromyzon*). Once again he achieved good results and received praise from Brücke.

V

Although he was at this time very much drawn to research it was not possible for him to continue for financial reasons. After graduating he had become engaged to Martha Bernays. In order to marry he must have more money and, in fact, as we have already seen, poverty was a longstanding problem. Brücke therefore advised him to leave the laboratory, and so he entered Vienna's principal hospital, soon becoming a junior resident physician. In his autobiography he admits that he was not attracted by the various branches of medicine proper, but only by psychiatry. Fortunately Dr. Theodore Meynert, whose lectures on psychiatry had impressed him as a student, was a member of the hospital staff. He had done impressive work on cerebral anatomy though he knew little of psychiatry in the modern sense. However Freud, still the rigid scientist, worked with him with

great concentration for about six months and studied the central
nervous system, this time of the human being. He concentrated
on the medulla oblongata, and notes that this work was in
complete contrast to the diffuse character of his studies during
his early years at the University before he had placed himself
under Brücke's discipline. In fact he was developing a decided
inclination to concentrate upon a single subject or problem, and
this tendency persisted to such an extent that he said it often led
to his being accused of one-sidedness.

VI

He was searching for deeper knowledge and more effective
methods in what he gradually came to be convinced was his
sphere of work, namely psychiatry. The great figure of the day
in this field was Charcot, whose remarkable and somewhat
theatrical work at the Salpêtrière was attracting unusual attention.
Freud was fortunate that, owing to a warm testimonial from
Brücke, he was awarded a travelling fellowship of considerable
value which enabled him to study in Paris under Charcot.

One of Charcot's important contributions to psychiatry was
to make the use of hypnotism acceptable in medical circles.
Three years before Freud went to Paris Charcot's work on hyp-
notic phenomena had been accepted by the French Academy of
Sciences. It was a new and stimulating world, and one that was
far removed from that of Brücke. It was indeed here that the
seeds of much of Freud's later work were sown; here, amongst
other places, that he received hints of a possible relationship
between sexual problems and neuroses; and here too that he
may have received certain insights into the dynamic nature of the
unconscious, although probably his visit to Bernheim was
more important in this respect.

He returned to Vienna after about six months in Paris and
set up as a consultant in nervous disorders. But when he reported
to the conservative Vienna Medical Society something of what
he had seen in Paris, as, for example, that hysteria was found in

men, he was greeted with scorn. Hypnotism might be accepted by the French Academy of Sciences but not by the Vienna Medical Society. Meynert added to the general ignominy with which he was treated by excluding him from his laboratory, saying that hypnosis was only a method for the artificial production of imbecility. Ultimately Freud was either forced out or absented himself from meetings of the learned medical societies and from academic life generally.

In order to appreciate what Freud finally accomplished we must consider the position of psychiatry when he began his work in Vienna. He says pathetically in his autobiography, "Anyone who wanted to make a living from the treatment of nervous patients must clearly be able to do something to help them".[16] Yet, as he states, his therapeutic arsenal contained only two weapons, electro-therapy and hypnotism, and he soon lost his faith in electro-therapy. Furthermore, he came to the conclusion that Erb's famous text-book on this subject, far from being an epitome of exact observations, was merely a fantasy. He described how painful it was for him to realize that the work of the greatest name in German neuro-pathology had no more relation to reality than some 'Egyptian' dream book of the kind which is sold in cheap bookshops. However, it helped him to rid himself of yet another part of the innocent faith in authority from which, he says, he was not yet free. He put his electric apparatus aside and later realized that any success which the application of electro-therapy had produced was solely the result of suggestion on the part of the physician. There was a stronger case for the use of hypnotism and so, after practising for five years, his principal instrument apart from haphazard and un-scientific therapeutic methods was hypnosis. Later, however, he discovered the drawbacks of this procedure. In addition to the fact that not all patients can be easily hypnotized, its results were frequently not lasting. Having heard of the remarkable work on hypnotism which was being done at Nancy he visited that city in the summer of 1889 and spent several weeks there. What impressed him more than anything else, although it was

less striking than the phenomena of hypnotism, was the possibility
that there are powerful mental processes which remain hidden
from consciousness.

VII

Gradually he produced the theories which have now become
so familiar and so influential. It was an astounding achievement.
Psychoanalysis was conceived by Freud and it came to vigorous
manhood during his lifetime. He had clearly found that for which
all his life he had been searching, consciously or unconsciously.
Yet, as Ernest Jones points out (p. 50), Brücke would have been
astonished, and that is putting it mildly, if he had known that
one of his favourite pupils was later, by his famous theory of
wish-fulfilment in the mind, to bring back into science such
ideas as 'purpose', 'intention' and 'aim', which he and members
of the Helmholtz school had considered banished for ever from
the universe. But, as Dr. Jones also points out, by the time that
Freud brought them back he was able to reconcile them with the
principles in which he had been brought up, for he never aban-
doned determinism for teleology.

VIII

Freud became an atheist at a very early age, so early indeed
that it is difficult to believe that he was mature enough, or that
he possessed sufficient knowledge, to justify such conclusions
against the general consensus of belief. When we remember that
he had always been made to feel, by his situation as a Jew in a
predominantly Catholic community, that he was permanently in
a minority his reaction is easy to understand, and if his father had
become a complete free-thinker (as his grandchildren claim) the
change would not be so great after all. Nevertheless, his atheism
does not seem to be so completely rational as he himself appeared
to think. It was adopted too early in life, and the nature of his
writings about religion lacks those qualities of objectivity and
calm which we find elsewhere in his books.

Many incidents reveal the development of his attitude towards religion. For instance, his mother-in-law, Emmeline Bernays, who was an intelligent and well-educated woman, had been brought up according to the strict rules of orthodox Judaism and she had reared Martha in the same way. This led to serious friction since Freud was bitterly opposed to what he regarded as pure superstition. According to Jewish custom Martha was not allowed to write on the Sabbath, so she used to write letters in pencil in the garden, rather than use a pen and write in the house where her mother would be able to see. This amazed Freud and he called Martha 'weak' for not standing up to her mother. His purpose was clear and he expressed it to Martha in the following words: "Eli [Martha's brother who after their father's death was the responsible male member of the family] little knows what a heathen I am going to make of you."[17] He was determined that Martha should give up her 'religious prejudices', and he succeeded, for she did give up her observance of the orthodox religious customs.

Her family naturally looked upon Freud as a heathen and would have preferred her to marry someone who was in the fold. One can imagine that his attitude to the wedding ceremonies did not endear him to them. There were great differences of opinion on this subject, for the usual kind of Jewish wedding was anathema to Freud, and he wanted his own to be as quiet and secret as possible. In discussing the marriage of his own sister, Anna, to Eli Bernays, Martha's brother, he wrote to Martha: "Will you willingly do without the ring, the presents, congratulations, the being stared at and criticized, even the wedding dress and the carriage that everyone gazes at and even the 'Ah' of admiration when you appear? You must of course have your own way in the matter: I dare not even show what I dislike, but I trust that our intentions will coincide."[18]

Ernest Jones writes: "He once went to a Jewish wedding, when his friend Paneth married Sophie Schwab. He gazed at the scene with a fascinated horror and then wrote a letter of sixteen pages describing all the odious detail in a spirit of malign mockery."[19]

In the end, however, he had to face a full Jewish marriage. He had hoped that a civil marriage would be sufficient, as in Germany, but in Austria a religious ceremony was necessary. Martha had made everything as easy as possible for him and arranged the wedding for a week-day when only a very few friends would be able to attend, and as it took place at her mother's house a silk hat and frock-coat would be worn instead of the more formal and customary evening dress.

Although religion played no part in his household, possibly even Freud forgot the unconscious which was far more powerful than his influence, for after he died and Martha was very old one of her greatest interests was to discuss Jewish customs and festivals with anyone who was interested in this subject. Perhaps we have here the "return of the repressed".

Another passage in Ernest Jones's *Life* is revealing: "The date of this fateful venture (his beginning in private practice) was Easter Sunday, April 25, 1886, a curious day to choose, since everything in Vienna was closed or suspended on that holy day. In a letter of April 12, 1936, he wrote, 'Easter Sunday signifies to me the fiftieth anniversary of taking up my medical practice'. It has been suggested that Easter had an emotional significance for him, dating from the Catholic Nanny who used to take him to the Church services in Freiberg, but to begin work on such a day *seems like an act of defiance*."[20]*

Freud's attitude towards religion even influenced his approach to art. In 1897 his friend Fliess suggested that he should see the great masterpieces of Italian art. He found, however, that his enjoyment was marred by the sacred, and especially the Christian, themes in the paintings.

IX

Probably the truth is that Freud was an iconoclast—indeed, unless he had been he would not have achieved the greatness which he undoubtedly did. He was prepared to break with medical tradition and he did so in his emphasis on the unconscious,

* The italics are mine—AUTHOR.

and in his theory on the aetiology of the neuroses. He broke
with traditional prudery in the place he gave to infantile sexuality,
and indeed the place of sexuality in general. He broke with the
traditions of his own race. He broke with friends, Breuer, Fliess
Jung, Adler, Stekel, Rank, although the fault was not always his.
He admitted that he needed a strong friend and someone to hate.
At times it would appear as if this hate sprang from his position
as a Jew. In the end the majority might hate him actively, and
indeed in 1938, at the end of his life, this appeared to be imminent
and he moved to England. He hated anti-Semitism and towards
his own race he was loyal if not loving. It is possible that his
hatred of their customs was a displacement of his hatred of the
position in society of the Jews. His attitude towards the Gentile
religion is revealed in a letter to Martha when she was his
fiancée. He discussed his neurasthenia and what he should do
about it. He decided that he would take life more easily and says:
"For the rest of my time in the hospital I will live like the Goys,
modestly, learning the ordinary things without striving after
discoveries or reaching to the depths."[21] Apparently he felt
superior, but if so there was no compelling reason to use the
term 'Goys' which is "a somewhat contemptuous term for
'Gentiles' ".[22] Contempt is a complex emotion compounded of
fear and envy and emotional rejection. The chief distinguishing
mark of the Goys was their religion. To hate this religion was to
show a supreme contempt for the Goys. Nor can this be wondered
at when we recall that those who took pride in being named
after Christ had frequently revealed so little of His spirit towards
those of His own race.

Take Vienna itself. There an atmosphere of anti-Semitism,
created by a population ninety per cent. of whom called themselves Christian, could not possibly endear that faith, nor indeed
religion itself, to someone like Freud. Yet this was his world and
he well realized how deeply rooted and of long standing this
racial antagonism was. There had been a 'Jewish question' for
hundreds of years, and once an Ecclesiastical Christian Synod
had decreed special distinguishing apparel for the Jews. The

spirit of the ghetto and pogroms still lingered. It was not until Freud himself was eleven that a new constitution granted the Jews equal rights with other citizens. But this by no means meant the end of anti-Semitism, and Freud describes in *An Autobiographical Study* what happened six years later.

When, in 1873, I first joined the University, I experienced some appreciable disappointments. Above all, I found that I was expected to feel myself inferior and an alien because I was a Jew. I refused absolutely to do the first of these things. I have never been able to see why I should feel ashamed of my descent or, as people were beginning to say, of my race. I put up, without much regret, with my non-acceptance into the community; for it seemed to me that in spite of this exclusion an active fellow-worker could not fail to find some nook or cranny in the framework of humanity. These first impressions at the University, however, had one consequence which was afterwards to prove important; for at an early age I was made familiar with the fate of being in the Opposition and of being put under the ban of the 'compact majority'. The foundations were thus laid for a certain degree of independence of judgment.[23]

Going back to earlier days still we can perhaps realize more fully what anti-Semitism must have meant for Freud, for we have his own description in *The Interpretation of Dreams*.[24] Significantly enough it is embodied in a series of dreams "based on the longing to go to Rome". He had realized the consequences of belonging to an alien race, and admits that he was forced by the anti-Semitic feeling among his class-mates to take a definite stand. When he analysed the dreams on his longing to visit Rome he recalled one of his most vivid youthful experiences. At the age of ten or twelve he was walking with his father who told him of an incident from his early days proving, so he said, that they were now living in happier days. As a young man he was walking one day along the street in the village in which

C

Sigmund had been born. He was well dressed and wearing a new fur cap. A Christian came up, knocked his cap into the mud and shouted "Jew, get off the pavement". Anxiously, Sigmund asked "And what did you do?" He never forgot the calm reply: "I went into the street and picked up the cap." It is worth noting that Sigmund's future hero was the Semitic general, Hannibal, who hated Rome and almost destroyed it. If he did not regard religious people as his enemies, we can be certain that he did not look upon them as his friends.

NOTES TO CHAPTER I

[1] Ernest Jones, *Sigmund Freud—Life and Work*, vol. I. London, Hogarth Press (1953), p. 22.

[2] *Ibid.*, p. 6.

[3] *Ibid.*, p. 22.

[4] *Ibid.*, p. 21.

[5] *Ibid.*, p. 13.

[6] *Ibid.*, p. 174.

[7] S. Freud, *An Autobiographical Study*, trans. James Strachey. London, Hogarth Press (1935), p.13.

[8] *Ibid.*, p. 13.

[9] *Ibid.*, p. 14.

[10] F. Wittels, *Sigmund Freud*, trans. Eden and Cedar Paul. London, George Allen & Unwin (1924), p. 20.

[11] S. Freud, *op. cit.*, p. 133.

[12] Ernest Jones, *op. cit.*, p. 33.

[13] *Ibid.*, p. 45.

[14] *Ibid.*, p. 45.

[15] S. Freud, *op. cit.*, p. 15.

[16] *Ibid.*, p. 26.

[17] Ernest Jones, *op. cit.*, p. 128.

[18] *Ibid.*, p. 154.

[19] *Ibid.*, p. 154.

[20] *Ibid.*, pp. 157-8.

[21] *Ibid.*, p. 187.

[22] *Ibid.*, p. 187 n.

[23] S. Freud, *op. cit.*, pp. 14-5.

[24] S. Freud, *The Interpretation of Dreams*, trans. A. A. Brill, revised edn. London, George Allen & Unwin (1937), pp. 195-6.

2

Religion and Obsessional Neurosis

"Neurosis is by no means only negative; it is also positive. Only a soulless rationalism could and does overlook this fact, supported by the narrowness of a purely materialistic philosophy of life. In reality, the neurosis contains the soul of the sick person, or at least a considerable part of it, and if the neurosis could be taken out like a decayed tooth, in the rationalistic way, then the patient would have gained nothing and lost something very important, as much as a thinker who loses his doubt of the truth of his conclusions, or a moral man who loses his temptations, or a courageous man who loses fear. For the neurotic to lose his neurosis is tantamount to losing his object in life, whereby life is robbed of its zest and meaning."

"Religions are psychotherapeutic systems in the most actual meaning of the word, and in the widest measure. They express the scope of the soul's problems in mighty images. They are the acknowledgment and recognition of the soul, and at the same time the revelation and manifestation of the nature of the soul."

C. G. JUNG, *Psychological Reflections.**

I

IN 1907 Freud, then aged fifty-one, published a paper on "Obsessive Acts and Religious Practices" in which he traced the resemblance between obsessive acts in neurotics "and those religious observances by means of which the faithful give expression to their piety". He was convinced that the insight which he had gained into the origin and meaning of neurotic obsessions and 'ceremonial' would enable him to draw inferences by analogy about the psychological processes governing religious practices. He was cautious in this his earliest writing on religious psychology as we see when we compare it with his later writing on the same

* Edited by Jolande Jacobi, pp. 84-5 and 298.

subject, to which he so constantly and almost compulsively returned. Yet his conclusion is clear enough. Religion is "a universal obsessional neurosis".

He began his article by pointing out that obsessional neurotics feel compelled to carry out a fixed 'ceremonial' in certain directions. To the onlooker the compulsive procedure appears meaningless and, in fact, at the conscious level, it is so to the neurotic himself. But if he does not obey the compulsive urge to perform these actions, he experiences intense anxiety.

Analysis reveals that these obsessive acts are only outwardly foolish and meaningless, because for the unconscious life of the obsessional they are full of meaning and serve important interests of the personality. They express the continuing influence of former experiences which have been repressed, but which are still heavily charged with emotion.

As an illustration of an obsessional neurotic Freud gives the following: "A woman who was living apart from her husband was subject to a compulsion to leave the best of whatever she ate; for example, she would only take the outside of a piece of roast meat. This renunciation was explained by the date of its origin. It appeared the day after she had refused marital relations with her husband, that is to say, had given up the best."[1]

II

Turning from his study of obsessional neurosis to examine religion Freud was struck by a number of resemblances between them. He first mentions three:

1. The fear of pangs of conscience following any omission of the neurotic's ceremonial, or the religious person's rite.
2. The complete isolation of both neurotic ceremonial and religious rites "from all other activities (and the feeling that one must not be disturbed)".
3. "The conscientiousness with which the details are carried out."

Scattered throughout the article five more resemblances are given:

4. Guilt.
5. Renunciations of instincts.
6. The element of compromise.
7. "Acts of penance" in religious practice and their counterparts in the obsessional neurosis.
8. The mechanism of psychical displacement.

III

He attached great importance to all the resemblances he mentioned, and stated that they enable us to "draw by analogy inferences about the psychological processes of religious life".[2] He began his paper by appealing to the analogy between "obsessive acts in neurotics and those religious observances by means of which the faithful give expression to their piety".[3] From this analogy he concluded that religion is fundamentally of the same nature as obsessional neurosis. Qualitatively, he maintained, they are of the same pathological nature. The 'ceremonial' of the obsessional neurotic cannot be taken at its face value; it has a meaning for the unconscious apart from which the obsessional symptoms are meaningless. The implication is that religion is in fact something other than it appears to be, namely a symbolic expression of the unconscious. It is "a universal obsessional neurosis".[4] Religion is not only simply explained but explained away. It is a pathological condition to be dispersed by analysis as soon as possible so that man, no longer hampered by its unhealthy influence, can move on to greater progress. However, tracing a resemblance is quite different from finding something identical. Two objects on the sea may have marked resemblances. They may be of the same size, shape and colour, and may both float in similar fashion; yet one is a lifebuoy and the other a mine. He ended by referring to these resemblances and analogies which make one "venture to regard the obsessional neurosis as a pathological counterpart to the formation of a religion, to describe this neurosis as a private religious system, and religion as a universal obsessional neurosis".[5]

No one, of course, could possibly claim that the realm of religion lies outside the operations of the obsessional neurotic. It would, therefore, be perfectly easy for any competent psychiatrist to point to the way in which some people carry out their religious observances, ceremonial or rites, and conclude that obsessional elements are present. There is a percentage of obsessional neurotics in the population, and as a very large percentage indeed of the total population believes in some form of religion, as Freud admitted when he called religion a universal obsessional neurosis, we should expect to find a certain percentage of obsessional neurotics among religious people. Their neuroses are quite as likely to affect their practice of religion as their housework. In actual fact obsessional symptoms are frequently related to the most important areas of life and we should therefore expect the obsessional neurotic to express his compulsiveness in his religion. A course of analysis would reveal evidence about the obsessional neurosis, but *not* about the truth or falsity of religion itself.

Freud went even further and asserted that religion itself was obsessional in nature. Are then the resemblances to which he referred so close and of such a nature that his conclusion is justified?

IV

The first resemblance is that both with neurotic ceremonial and religious rites there is a fear of pangs of conscience after their omission. It is questionable, however, if the suffering of the obsessional should be called pangs of conscience. He experiences extreme anxiety, the feeling that an indefinite, indefinable calamity is threatening him. He finds it extremely difficult to describe his sufferings, and they vary considerably according to the nature of the unconscious conflict which causes them. But what he feels is not, properly speaking, pangs of conscience at all, it is pathological anxiety. Some religious people of an obsessional nature experience this about some parts of their religious observances or rites, as indeed they do about what they conceive to be their religious duties.

Conscience is much more closely related to our conscious life than to our unconscious. The obsessional, whether religious or not, will, in so far as he is behaving in an obsessional way, suffer no pangs of conscience. This term, whether applied to the religious or the irreligious, should be confined to behaviour governed by conscious motivation.

Any priest, minister or rabbi would confirm that many members of his congregation can omit their religious rites without suffering pangs of conscience. A proportion, and amongst them the obsessionals, will feel uneasy, but the majority will treat their religious omissions in the same rational way as they treat omissions in other parts of their life. If these fears were as widely present as Freud assumed, religious ceremonies would be much better attended than in fact they are.

V

The second resemblance is "in the complete isolation of them [neurotic ceremonial and religious rites] from all other activities (the feeling that one must not be disturbed)".[6] This is clearly a symptom of the type of neurotic ceremonial which Freud describes, for it appears to be as meaningless to the onlooker as it does to the patient himself. But the religious person does not ordinarily isolate his rites and his religion from all other activities, as the Hindu and Mohammedan prove when they pray in public. On the contrary, he would claim that this is the last thing he ought or wants to do. For some Christians the bread and wine in the central rite of their faith are significant because they symbolize primary elements in the natural order, and are related to the everyday activities which produce them. Religious bodies almost without exception prepare candidates for full membership by doing the very opposite of what Freud described as a characteristic of religious rites: they attempt to make sure that candidates fully understand the meaning of all rites and relate them to other activities. The obsessional neurotic does not like to be disturbed during his meaningless and puzzling ceremonial, whereas religious rites are rarely practised alone.

VI

Freud's third resemblance was "the conscientiousness with which the details are carried out".[7] Once again there is an unfortunate use of terminology. It is compulsiveness rather than conscientiousness which the obsessional neurotic displays. Describing the symptoms in the obsessional Freud wrote: "He is quite incapable of renouncing them, for every neglect of the ceremonial is punished with the most intolerable anxiety, which forces him to perform it instantly."[8] The Shorter Oxford Dictionary defines conscientiousness as "loyalty to conscience", and conscience as "internal conviction . . . the internal recognition of the moral quality of one's motives and actions; the faculty or principle which pronounces upon the moral quality of one's actions or motives, approving the right and condemning the wrong." To be conscientious, according to the same authority, means to be "habitually governed by a sense of duty". The moral quality cannot be avoided if 'conscientiousness' is used. So that although this term is appropriate for a large part of religious life, it is not a correct description when applied to the way in which "the details may be carried out". Exaggerated 'pangs of conscience' are condemned in most forms of religious practice under the heading of scrupulosity.

VII

The fourth resemblance is guilt: " . . . a sufferer from compulsions and prohibitions behaves as if he were dominated by a sense of guilt, of which, however, he is ignorant—an unconscious sense of guilt, as one must call it in spite of the apparent contradiction in terms."[9] The neurotic ceremonial is a protective measure,

an act of defence intended to ward off punishment. "The protestations of the pious that they know they are miserable sinners in
their hearts correspond to the sense of guilt of the obsessional
neurotic; while the pious observances (prayers, invocations, etc.)
with which they begin every act of the day, and especially every
unusual undertaking, seem to have the significance of defensive
and protective measures."[10]

Freud missed the vital point about prayers such as the General
Confession in the Anglican Church, namely that it is an open
statement by the sinner that he is well aware of the fact that he is
a sinner and a miserable one; that he knows that he has done
those things which he ought not to have done and left undone
those things which he ought to have done. His act of confession is,
above everything else, a conscious one and everything is done
by the religious community to make it as conscious as possible.
Ordinarily there are preparatory sentences and a solemn calling
upon the believer to examine himself before he makes his confession. Thus according to strict Freudian theory this resemblance
breaks down, and a fundamental difference arises in its place,
that between an unconscious process and a conscious one. We
have, in fact, on the one hand an unhealthy pathological guilt,
and on the other a healthy self-knowledge, the result of self-
analysis, possibly with the assistance of priest or minister.

Freud created his resemblances: they were not present in his
material. This is clearly shown by his reference to "the pious
observances (prayer, invocations, etc.) with which they begin
every act of the day, and especially every unusual undertaking,
seem to have the significance of defensive and protective
measures."[11] Although this might seem to have the significance
of defensive and protective measures and so resemble neurotic
ceremonial, it is surely a very unreal representation of the behaviour of religious people. Some attach little importance to these
kinds of observance, and many others who may regard them as
important nevertheless in actual practice neglect them.

VIII

A fifth resemblance is the one which Freud considered the most important and about which he has most to say. "The essential resemblance would lie in the fundamental renunciation of the satisfaction of inherent instincts, and the chief difference in the nature of these instincts, which in the neurosis are exclusively sexual, but in religion are of egoistic origin."[12] In explaining the nature of the instincts which are renounced in religion he said that they "are egoistic, antisocial instincts, though even these for the most part are not without a sexual element".[13]

He regarded the symptoms of obsessional neurosis as a sub-stitute satisfaction for the renunciation of the sexual instincts, and the phenomena of religion as due to the renunciation of the egoistic and antisocial instincts. There is here the suggestion that just as one renunciation of the instincts leads to all the symptoms of obsessional neurosis and so is clearly unhealthy, so religion is of the same nature: it is a "universal obsessional neurosis". But Freud was confused on this point for he stated on page 34: "A progressive renunciation of inherent instincts, the satisfaction of which is capable of giving direct pleasure to the ego, appears to be one of the foundations of human civilization".[14] Therefore, as he certainly regarded the foundation of human civilization as good and desirable, there must be a place for some renunciation of inherent instincts, especially of the egoistic and antisocial ones. Thus according to his own finding about this essential resem-blance, religion has a vital function to perform in the foundation of human civilization.

Whether he was correct in thinking that the repression of certain instinctual trends is one of the foundations on which religion is built, or whether religion on the contrary shows the way to the full flowering of the instincts as others would claim, he was surely incorrect in claiming that it is the "sole" foundation on which religion is built. This is too narrow an approach to religious phenomena which include traditional, moral, affective and rational elements. Freud underrated the place of the conscious activities of the mind in the religious structure, and he did not explain why the repression of instinctual trends leads to belief in religion itself, in the many different forms which it takes.

IX

The sixth resemblance lies in the element of compromise which he believed to be present both in obsessional ceremonials and religious practices. An obsessional act is a compromise in that it is a defence against temptation and also a substitute or symbolical satisfaction of the original impulse. He was hard put to it to find a resemblance here, for "the element of compromise in those obsessive acts which we find in neurotic symptoms is the feature least easy to find reproduced in corresponding religious observances."[15] His argument is very unreal, and the compromise is found in an attempt to show that the very instincts which religion represses "are yet committed precisely in the name of, and ostensibly in the cause of, religion".[16] One illustration is given to show that individuals are required to sacrifice "the satisfaction of their instincts to the divinity".[17] It is a quotation from the Bible torn from its context, "Vengeance is Mine, saith the Lord". The complete verse, given in Romans xii. 19-21, reads "Dearly beloved, avenge not yourselves, but rather give place unto wrath: for it is written, Vengeance is Mine; I will repay, saith the Lord. Therefore if thine enemy hunger, feed him; if he thirst, give him drink: for in so doing thou shalt heap coals of fire on his head. Be not overcome of evil, but overcome evil with good." The meaning of this passage is that the Christian believer can leave the establishment of righteousness to the One Who is righteous, God Himself, for the God Whose will it is that His followers shall overcome evil with good would not do less Himself.

X

In dealing with the seventh resemblance Freud wrote: "unredeemed backslidings into sin are even more common among the pious than among neurotics, and these give rise to a new form of religious activity, namely, the acts of penance of which one finds counterparts in the obsessional neurosis."[18] These counterparts are the acts of defence or security which form part of the protective measures in the ceremonial of the obsessional neurotic. Apart from the fact that no evidence is produced for the statement that there are more unredeemed backslidings into sin among the pious than among neurotics, this statement, even if true, does not appear to have the slightest relevance. There is, however, the vast difference that acts of penance are conscious ones whereas the ceremonial of the neurotic is an activity of the unconscious. Only if the term 'acts of penance' is used in a very loose sense would it be possible for them to form part of the ceremonial of an obsessional neurotic. And it is untrue to say that acts of penance are always a protective measure, an act of defence or security. Their quality varies greatly. They may be a protective measure designed to ward off the wrath of an unreasonable tribal god, or they may express sorrow because the sinner believes that he has sinned against a loving God.

XI

The eighth and last resemblance is what Freud called "the mechanism of psychical displacement", and he wrote: "It cannot be denied that in the religious sphere also there is a similar tendency to a displacement of psychical values, and indeed in the same direction, so that petty ceremonials gradually become the essence of religious practices, and replace the ideas underlying them. It is for this reason that religions are subject to retroactive reforms which aim at the re-establishment of the original relative values."[19] As most religious communities clearly recognize, this possibility exists and it is prone to affect obsessionals who are religious. It is something which a very large number of religious people try to guard against. Freud went much too far in asserting that petty ceremonials gradually become the essence of practices. Because this may happen with individuals from time to time is no reason for drawing a generalization about the nature of religious practices as a whole. It is unfortunate that he did not pay heed to his own admissions in his reference to the ideas underlying religious practices, and also to the retroactive reforms which aim at the re-establishment of the original relative values. There can be a process or mechanism of psychical displacement in the realm of religion, but that is not religion itself.

XII

Freud recognized that there are differences between obsessional neurosis and religion and began by mentioning three:

1. The greater individual variability of neurotic ceremonial in contrast to the stereotyped character of rites (prayer, orientations, etc.).
2. Its private nature as opposed to the public and communal character of religious observances.
3. That whereas small details of religious ceremonies are full of meaning and are understood symbolically, those of neurotics seem silly and meaningless. In this respect an obsessional neurosis furnishes a tragi-comic travesty of a private religion.

Freud added another difference later in his article: the nature of the instincts involved.

These four differences which he distinguished between the ceremonial of the obsessional neurotic and the practices of religious people are no more convincing than his resemblances.

The first difference is the greater individual variability of neurotic ceremonial in contrast to the stereotyped character of rites (prayer, orientations, etc.). He was, of course, correct in referring to the difference in the ceremonial followed by the individual obsessional neurotic. When analysed, the symptoms can be seen to have a distinct individual basis. They may be appropriate to the psychological condition of that one individual. But there are certain types of obsessional actions and, in fact, he mentioned a number of them in this article. There is a whole class connected with "dressing and undressing, going to bed, and the satisfaction of bodily needs".[20] Another form is connected with locking up at night. But the performance of religious rites is less stereotyped than Freud thought. To begin with there is a list of almost numberless rites which can be followed, and the choice and manner in which they are practised are extremely varied. He did not make sufficient allowance either for the various types of obsessional practices which are to be found, or for the individual variations in the carrying out of religious practices.

XIII

The second difference is also unconvincing, for the contrast between private and public is far too sharp in Freud's statement that the private nature of the obsessional neurotic's ceremonial differs from the public and communal nature of religious observances. Undoubtedly neurotic ceremonial is largely of a private nature and thus different from religion, which often has a public and communal character as well. Indeed, there is little meaning in this difference, because of his insistence on the fact that the private nature of the neurotic's ceremonial means little since the neurotic does not grasp what is really happening, because the real causes of his behaviour are unconscious. Therefore, Freud is saying little if anything more than that the neurotic is acting as an individual, whereas there is a public and communal aspect to religious observances, yet prayer and much else in the religious life are just as individual.

XIV

There is one difference which Freud mentioned as outstanding: "the distinction that the little details of religious ceremonies are full of meaning and are understood symbolically, while those of neurotics seem silly and meaningless. In this respect an obsessional neurosis furnishes a tragi-comic travesty of a private religion."[21] He thought that much of this apparent difference is dissolved when we see that obsessive acts are full of meaning for the unconscious. He even took back his admission later in his article that we have here an outstanding difference, and said: "We must remember that as a rule the ordinary religious observer carries out a ceremonial without concerning himself with its significance, although priests and investigators may be familiar with its meaning, which is usually symbolic. In all believers, however, the *motives* impelling them to religious practices are unknown, or are replaced in consciousness by others which are advanced in their stead."[22] Freud could not possibly know or demonstrate that the ordinary religious observer carries out a ceremonial without being aware of its significance. This is an unproved generalization. Even if it were true it would still leave unexplained the observances of those priests and investigators who are familiar with the meaning. Nor could he possibly know that the motives of all other religious believers are unknown to them.

<h2 style="text-align:center">XV</h2>

The last difference mentioned by Freud concerns the nature of the instincts involved. With the obsessional neurotic there is a renunciation of the sexual instinct, whereas with the religious life it is the egoistic, antisocial instincts that are concerned. Such a distinction, however, cannot be supported, and the attempt to make it recalls the old-fashioned, atomistic approach to the emotional life of the individual. The functioning of instincts cannot be distinguished in this way, and in fact there is now considerable reluctance among psychologists to make a list of the instincts. There may be sexual elements as well as what Freud attempted to distinguish as egoistic elements in the lives and symptoms both of the obsessional and of the religious individual.

<h2 style="text-align:center">XVI</h2>

In the article under consideration Freud had a sure touch in discussing obsessional neurosis, and his observations were

startlingly original in 1907. But he was less happy in his treatment
of religion. He had already made contributions of importance
to the study of obsessional neurosis, and the chief interest of this
article is the light it throws on his conception of religion and the
religious believer. The very title, "Obsessive Acts and Religious
Practices", reveals his approach. His first sentence referred to
"those religious observances by means of which the faithful give
expression to their piety".[23] He was convinced that the general
resemblance between obsessive acts and religious practices is a
close one. He also wrote of "the resemblance between neurotic
ceremonial and religious rites".[24] Religion for him consisted of
practices, observances, rites and ceremonial. These undoubtedly
are a part of the religious life, but Freud treated them as the
subject matter of religion itself. And as the religious practices,
observances and rites appeared to him closely to resemble the
ceremonial of the obsessional neurotic they could be explained
as symbols and accounted for by psychical displacement in
exactly the same way. Both sets of symptoms have their roots
in the unconscious, and because of this the explanations, interpretations and apparent meanings which are given to them at
merely conscious levels cannot be taken seriously.

XVII

Freud approached his study of religion with very definite
assumptions, for he had come to the conclusion long before he
used the word in his writings that it was an illusion. Inevitably
he looked at religion from the outside and concentrated on
religious practices, observances and rites, and in fact appeared to
equate religion with them. He could see that religious people
believed in what they were doing and if they were mistaken, as
he was convinced they were, the true reasons for their actions
were hidden from them and lay deep in the unconscious. He
never appeared to question whether or not he had grasped the
whole content of religion as it is experienced by those who
believe in it. One conclusion, however, was ruled out and

indeed was not even considered: that the practices, observances, rites and beliefs of the religious might be justified by their correspondence with reality. If an investigator firmly rules out one explanation from the very beginning, he will not find it even if it is there.

XVIII

Nowhere in this article did he define religion, although he revealed very clearly his own attitude. It is largely a matter of practices, observances, ceremonials and rites, and can be summed up as "a universal obsessional neurosis".[25] This is a narrow approach to the very varied phenomena of religion. Freud was too much influenced by his early surroundings in the narrow world of Freiberg where ninety-six per cent. of the population were Roman Catholics and two per cent. were Jews, and later by his life in Vienna where the same forms of religion were to be found. Unfortunately he does not appear to have studied, except in the superficial way of *Totem and Taboo*, the widely differing forms which religion has taken. His conclusions might well have been otherwise had he considered the nature of primitive religions, or even the fulminations of the great prophets such as Amos and Isaiah against a religion of mere rites and observances. If he had moved about the world with open eyes he would surely have been impressed by the variety of the forms taken by religion. He would have found Quakers, Congregationalists, Baptists, Episcopalians, Methodists and a host of smaller communities. A careful study of Roman Catholicism itself would have revealed the considerable differences between the religious orders such as Jesuits, Dominicans, Franciscans, Benedictines, Capuchins and so on, which all have their place in that Church. He would also have discovered that a number of communities, and certainly a large number of religious people, had little use for religious rites. In some forms the emphasis is on a philosophy of life, on beliefs about the nature of the universe, of man and of God. Many religious people have been as well aware as he was of the existence of the unconscious, and have studied as honestly as he

D

its influence on their religious practices and beliefs, and have emerged with a religion which they maintain is all the stronger and healthier for this examination. It is difficult to imagine that this great concourse represents no more than the procedure of the obsessional neurotic, and Freud only succeeded in doing so by holding firmly to a narrow picture of religion consisting almost entirely of a number of stereotyped rites the meaning of which was hidden from the participants. It is a neat theory but it is remarkably unsatisfactory as an explanation of the nature of concepts and experiences so infinitely varied and so powerfully persistent as those which constitute religion.

XIX

In calling religion "a universal mass neurosis" Freud is referring to something very different from what the psychiatrist understands by obsessional neurosis when he meets it in his consulting room. There it emerges as individual and abnormal, whereas religion is universal and therefore normal, and it is a misuse of terms to call it a neurosis. What Freud really meant was that although religion is universal it nevertheless resembles the ceremonial of the obsessional neurotic. But there is the important distinction that one is normal and the other is not, and the normal should be looked at much more carefully, because merely to call it pathological does not make it so. It may be healthy and true.

Even if Freud had succeeded in tracing the motives in the unconscious which lead to certain forms of religion he would not have disposed of religion itself. In actual practice, however, it is extremely difficult to be sure that the real motives have been adequately traced. Even if some motives have been found, they may be accounted for by others; or possibly only some of the motives may have been found, and these not by any means the most important. Whatever motives may or may not be laid bare, the issue of validity has to be approached in an entirely different way. The evidence for or against the validity of religion or psychoanalysis or any other system of thought has to be examined in appropriate ways. Belief or faith may be responsible in the last resort for a personal decision on whether or not to treat something as valid. And this way of faith or belief is in fact the one followed by Freud. He believed in the reasonableness of psychoanalysis and he had faith in atheism, although from the very nature of the subject matter he could not prove that he was right. He attempted to demolish religion by tracing the motives on which he thought it was based in particular cases, and his own atheism was open to precisely the same form of attack. This approach establishes nothing. That is why Freud's article leaves religion exactly where it was before. It would have been wiser to live and let live, and allow the issue of validity to be decided by methods which are appropriate and fitting to that particular subject.

NOTES TO CHAPTER 2

[1] S. Freud, "Obsessive Acts and Religious Practices" (1907), in *Collected Papers*, vol. II. London, Hogarth Press (1924), pp. 28-9.
[2] *Ibid.*, p. 25.
[3] *Ibid.*, p. 25.
[4] *Ibid.*, p. 34.
[5] *Ibid.*, p. 34.
[6] *Ibid.*, p. 27.
[7] *Ibid.*, p. 27.
[8] *Ibid.*, p. 26.
[9] *Ibid.*, p. 31.
[10] *Ibid.*, p. 31.
[11] *Ibid.*, p. 31.
[12] *Ibid.*, p. 34.
[13] *Ibid.*, p. 33.
[14] *Ibid.*, p. 34.
[15] *Ibid.*, p. 34.
[16] *Ibid.*, p. 34.
[17] *Ibid.*, p. 34.
[18] *Ibid.*, p. 33.
[19] *Ibid.*, p. 34.
[20] *Ibid.*, p. 26.
[21] *Ibid.*, pp. 27-8.
[22] *Ibid.*, pp. 30-1.
[23] *Ibid.*, p. 25.
[24] *Ibid.*, p. 27.
[25] *Ibid.*, p. 34.

3

"In the Beginning . . ."

"I still adhere to this sequence of thought. I have often been vehemently reproached for not changing my opinions in later editions of my book, since more recent ethnologists have without exception discarded Robertson Smith's theories and have in part replaced them by others which differ extensively. I would reply that these alleged advances in science are well known to me. Yet I have not been convinced either of their correctness or of Robertson Smith's errors. Contradiction is not always refutation; a new theory does not necessarily denote progress. Above all, however, I am not an ethnologist, but a psychoanalyst. It was my good right to select from ethnological data what would serve me for my analytic work. The writings of the highly gifted Robertson Smith provided me with valuable points of contact with the psychological material of analysis and suggestions for the use of it. I cannot say the same of the work of his opponents."

SIGMUND FREUD, *Moses and Monotheism* (p. 207).

I

IN 1912 Freud, following the lead of Jung,[1] began to study the behaviour of primitive peoples, especially with regard to the subjects of totem and taboo. He later asserted in *An Autobiographical Study*[2] that he placed a high value upon his contribution to the psychology of religion, and it is this theme which dominates his *Totem and Taboo*.

Most of the book is concerned with the phenomena of totem and taboo themselves, and on the basis of what Freud believed to be their significance he deduced important conclusions about the nature of religious experience. His deductions, however, are entirely dependent on the conclusions that he came to in his study of the anthropological material relating to totem and taboo. So of necessity the validity of his conclusions stands or falls on whether he was right or wrong in his anthropological

observations. We must concern ourselves, therefore, first with
Freud's claims about the origin and nature of totem and taboo,
and secondly with the evidence now available on these subjects,
and the conclusions of competent anthropologists. If, after a
consideration of these matters, we come to the conclusion that
Freud's treatment of the origin and significance of totem and
taboo is unsound, then the superstructure concerning the nature
of religion which he built up will have little significance or
interest, and need not occupy much of our time.

What exactly was Freud's view as given in this work?
He develops it along the following lines: the dread of incest
is stronger among primitive people than among civilized races,
and special precautions are taken against its occurrence. Then he
examined the relation between the prohibitions demanded by
systems of taboo which he regarded as the earliest form of moral
restrictions, and the experience of emotional ambivalence. By
the latter term, he meant that there are commonly two aspects
when emotion is experienced towards anyone, namely love and
hate. Freud also claimed to find in the primitive scheme of the
universe known as animism, a principle "of the overestimation
of the importance of psychical reality. . . ." He called this the
principle of "the omnipotence of thought", and he regarded
it as the root of magic. The existence of this principle means
that primitive peoples find it difficult to separate thought from
reality, and, in this, they are like very young children. He was
also very much interested in totemism and looked upon it as
the first system or organization in primitive tribes, a system in
which the beginnings of social order are connected with elemen-
tary forms of religion and domination by a small number of
taboo prohibitions.

In the summary of *Totem and Taboo* given in *An Autobiographical
Study* (1925) Freud wrote: "The being that is honoured is ultimately always an animal, from which the clan also claims to be
descended."[3] In *Totem and Taboo*, however, he does not go so far
as this: "Now what is a totem? As a rule it is an animal, either

edible and harmless, or dangerous and feared; more rarely the
totem is a plant or a force of nature (rain, water), which stands in
a peculiar relation to the whole clan."[4] He claimed that even
the most highly developed races had once passed through the
stage of totemism.

The chief literary sources for these theories were the works
of Sir James Frazer, and especially his *Totemism and Exogamy* and
The Golden Bough. He considered, however, that although Frazer
gave the facts he did not solve the problems of totemism, pointing
out that Frazer had altered his views on this subject several times
in a fundamental way, and also that other ethnologists and prehistorians were uncertain and in disagreement. What Freud
accepted as the clue to understanding the problems was the
striking correspondence between the two main taboo prohibitions
of totemism—"not to kill the totem" and "not to have sexual
relations with any woman of the same totem clan", and "the
two elements of the Oedipus complex",[5] namely the killing of
the father and the taking of the mother as wife. Because of this
correspondence he was "tempted to equate the totem animal
with the father".[6] He claimed that primitive people do this
quite clearly when they honour the totem animal as the forefather
of the clan. Two facts gleaned from psychoanalysis were of vital
importance, the first being what he called "a lucky observation"[7]
of a child which Ferenczi had made and which pointed to an
"infantile return of totemism".[8] The other was found through
the analysis of the early animal phobias in children which were
thought to show that the animal was a substitute for the father.
This substitute was derived by displacement from the Oedipus
complex and represented the fear of the father. Freud reached
the conclusion that "not much was lacking to enable me to
recognize the killing of the father as the nucleus of totemism and
the starting point in the formation of religion".[9]

He believed that he had found what was lacking in W.
Robertson Smith's work *The Religion of the Semites*, where the
author expressed his view that the totem feast was an essential
part of the totemistic religion. Once every year the totem

animal, which at all other times was regarded as sacred, was solemnly killed in the presence of all the clan, was then devoured, and afterwards mourned over. Later there followed a great festival.

II

Another part of Freud's theory was derived from Darwin's conjecture that originally men lived in hordes and that each person was under the domination of a single, powerful, violent and jealous male. Perhaps we are going far even in using the term theory; for Freud himself, in describing the influences which had formed his opinion, said that as he considered all these components there arose before him "the following hypothesis, or, I would rather say, vision",[10] and this hypothesis or vision was the very heart of the thesis he set forward in *Totem and Taboo*.

He believed that in this primal horde the father, being all-powerful, seized all the women for himself, and either drove away or killed his sons because they were potentially dangerous rivals. Then he states "one day, however, the sons came together and united to overwhelm, kill, and devour their father, who had been their enemy but also their ideal".[11] Because of the potential rivalry among themselves they were unable to take over their heritage. Through the combined influences of failure and regret they had to learn to come to an agreement among themselves, and so they formed a clan and, in this, the practices of totemism had their place. The main purpose of this totemism was to prevent the repetition of such a deed, and they all undertook to forego the possession of the women for whom they had killed their father. They were then driven to find women elsewhere and this was the origin of the exogamy which is so closely bound up with totemism. The totem feast commemorated the fearful deed which was the source of man's sense of guilt or 'original sin'. Here also he claimed to find "the beginning, at once, of social organization, of religion and of ethical restrictions".[12]

His hypothesis continued thus: after a time the totem animal no longer was a substitute for the primal father who had been both "feared and hated, honoured and envied",[13] and he then became "the prototype of God himself".[14] The son's rebellion against his father, combined with his affection for him, produced in the course of time various compromises, the purpose of which was to atone for the original act of parricide. Freud believed that his view revealed the psychological basis of Christianity in which he maintained the ceremony of the totem feast still survives "with but little distortion, in the form of Communion".[15]

III

The opening paragraph in Chapter 4 of *Totem and Taboo* on "The Infantile Recurrence of Totemism" suggests a cautious approach, for he states definitely, and indeed wisely: "The reader need not fear that psychoanalysis, which first revealed the regular over-determination of psychic acts and formations, will be tempted to derive anything so complicated as religion from a single source. If it necessarily seeks, as in duty bound, to gain recognition for one of the sources of this institution, it by no means claims exclusiveness for this source or even first rank among the concurring factors. Only a synthesis from various fields of research can decide what relative importance in the genesis of religion is to be assigned to the mechanism which we are to discuss; but such a task exceeds the means as well as the intentions of the psychoanalyst."[16] In the chapter itself, however, he appeared to forget this qualification and developed elaborately the theme outlined above.

In his development he considered how concepts of God came into relation with totemism. His answer was that the idea of God appeared, but no one knew whence, and it gradually dominated the whole religious life and the totem feast had to fit itself, if it were to survive, into the new system. Here again, he did not examine the anthropological material dispassionately, but simply stated: "However, psychoanalytic investigation of the individual teaches with especial emphasis that god is in every case modelled after the father and that our personal relation to god is dependent upon our relation to our physical father, fluctuating and changing with him, and that god at bottom is nothing but an exalted father."[17] Soon afterwards, however, comes one of his rare words of caution: "If psychoanalysis deserves any consideration at all, then the share of the father in the idea of a god must be very important, quite aside from all the other origins and meanings of god upon which psychoanalysis can throw no light."[18]

Freud touched on one particular difficulty only to pass it over. He knew that at certain periods and among certain tribes there were maternal deities, and believed that these everywhere preceded the paternal deities. But he did not face the implication of such facts and their effect on his hypothesis.

He paid particular attention to Christianity, maintaining that it was one way of dealing with the sense of guilt which was ultimately derived from the primal crime. The way which Christ took was to sacrifice His own life and through this redeem His brothers from primal sin. In the Christian myth (and he assumed that it is a myth) man's original sin was undoubtedly an offence against God the Father. The fact that Christ redeemed mankind from the weight of original sin through the sacrifice of His own life could only mean that this sin was none other than murder. The law of retaliation which is deeply rooted in human feeling demands that a murder can only be atoned for by the sacrifice of another life. Such self-sacrifice points to a blood guilt. If the sacrifice of a life brings about the reconciliation with God the Father, then the crime which has to be expiated can only be the murder of the father: "Thus, in the Christian doctrine mankind most unreservedly acknowledges the guilty deed of primordial times because it now has found the most complete expiation for this deed in the sacrificial death of the son. The reconciliation with the father is the more thorough because simultaneously with this sacrifice there follows the complete renunciation of woman for whose sake mankind rebelled against the father."[19]

Freud carried his argument further by pointing out that such are the demands made through the principle of ambivalence that, by the same deed which made the greatest expiation possible to the father, the son also satisfies his wishes against the father. He does this by becoming "a god himself beside or rather in place of his father. The religion of the son succeeds the religion of the father."[20] That this substitution takes place is revealed by the revival of the old totem feast in the form of communion in which the modern band of brothers eats and drinks the flesh and blood of the son instead of those of the father. In this way the sons identify themselves with the son and themselves become holy. Freud states explicitly: "At bottom, however, the Christian communion is a new setting aside of the father, a repetition of the crime that must be expiated. We see how well justified is Frazer's dictum that 'the Christian communion has absorbed within itself a sacrament which is doubtless far older than Christianity'."[21] Another essential part of Freud's theory is his conclusion that the beginnings of religion, ethics, society and art meet in the Oedipus complex.

He believed that all these cultural phenomena came about as reactions to the primal misdeed which, in the end, gave those who carried it out the conception of crime. It gave rise to the first crime and consequent moral restrictions in primal society. Those who had committed this crime regretted it and determined that it should not be repeated, nor should its actual occurrence be allowed to bring any gain. Here especially, Freud maintained, we have the beginning of that creative sense of guilt which is still with us. In neurotics it has antisocial effects by creating new rules of morality and continued restrictions which are produced unconsciously as an expiation for misdeeds committed, or as precautions against any misdeeds which are likely to be committed in the future. In neurotics we do not find the deeds but the impulses and feelings which would tend towards the deeds. In practice the neurotic is inhibited as far as the deeds are concerned. He exalts the psychic reality above the actual one, and reacts to thoughts as a normal person reacts towards realities. Freud claimed that in primitive man there is the same sense of psychic reality. In contrast to the practices of the neurotic the deed is not inhibited but is, in fact, a substitute for the thought, and thus Freud's concluding words in *Totem and Taboo* are reminiscent of the opening words of St. John's Gospel: "In the beginning was the deed".[22]

IV

This concluding sentence, "In the beginning was the deed", is fitting as far as his theories are concerned. The foundation of his argument lies in his comments about the primal horde. It was his key to the understanding of the phenomena connected with totem and taboo, the beginnings of culture and conscience. It was this deed which created as its permanent heritage the Oedipus complex, compounded as it is of the two desires: to kill the father and possess the mother. Hence Freud could write: "I want to state the conclusion that the beginnings of religion, ethics, society, and art meet in the Oedipus complex."[23] So much then depended on the foundation of the primal horde that its existence could admit of no doubt. To be of value it *must* have been the condition under which primitive man existed. Anthropologists have constantly investigated primitive tribes which might be expected to preserve ancient conditions, and prehistorians have searched the past, but none has found the conditions surmised by Freud. Freud himself admits that "this primal state of society has nowhere been observed".[24] Thus he wrote: "Now whether we suppose that such a possibility was a historical event or not, it brings the formation of religion within the circle of the father-complex and bases it upon the ambivalence which dominates that complex."[25]

As we have already observed, he relied mainly on "the well-known works of J. G. Frazer [*Totemism and Exogamy* and *The Golden Bough*], a mine of valuable facts and opinions".[26] Since he had in fact no first-hand knowledge of any society but his own, he was entirely dependent on secondary sources, and selected what appeared to support his theories in general. In this case it was the Oedipus complex. He also searched for evidence of origins; it was this which made him seize on what he thought was the Darwinian conjecture. Most anthropologists have now given up the search for origins because certainty in that realm is unattainable even for the practices of totem and taboo.

V

The soundness or otherwise of Freudian theories on totem and taboo was investigated by Malinowski who studied the Trobriand Islanders of Melanesia, and his work is of especial interest because he began as a sympathizer with psychoanalysis—possibly 'supporter' would not be too strong a word. He deals thoroughly with these theories, especially in *Sex and Repression in Savage Society* (1927). What is especially interesting in his findings is that they were based on a study of a matrilineal family system. At the beginning he thought that he could find general support for some of the psychoanalytical theories, but as time went on his views changed, and in Part III of this book *Sex and Repression in Savage Society*, which was written later, he became critical of Freud. In Chapter 3 he dealt specifically with *Totem and Taboo*, pointing out that psychoanalysts have always regarded the Oedipus complex as a source of culture. In *Totem and Taboo* Freud was trying to give the hypothesis which he believed actually accounted for its existence before the beginnings of culture. Malinowski's criticism of Freud was on the following grounds: in the passage from Darwin on which Freud built so much, Darwin was speaking about man and gorillas in an indiscriminate fashion. Malinowski believed that Freud failed to distinguish between the family as it occurs among the anthropoid apes and the organized human family, and it is, of course, all-important to discriminate between animal life in the state of nature and human life in culture. Darwin, in his passage, was developing an argument against the view of primitive sexual promiscuity, and so the distinction between the different types of family did not matter. If he had been dealing with the origins of culture and had attempted to fix the moment of its birth then the distinction between nature and culture would have been highly significant. Darwin also wrote about the wives of the leader of the herd and did not mention any other families. He also went on to point out that the young males who were shut out from the primal horde succeeded in finding other partners and so did not appear to trouble any more about the original horde.

As Malinowski points out, Freud substantially modified the Darwinian hypothesis. He insisted that the slaying of the father was the origin of human culture. Yet in his description he spoke about "some advance in culture", and "the use of a new weapon". From this it would appear that, at this time, a substantial store of culture, and indeed weapons, already existed.

He also described how the sons immediately after the murder of their father laid down laws and religious taboos and began forms of social organization. He claimed that they produced forms of culture which were to be handed on to future generations. Malinowski argued forcibly that if the raw material of culture existed already it is obvious "that the great event could not have created culture as it is supposed by Freud to have done".[27] On the other hand, if culture at the time of the deed did not exist, the sons could not have immediately instituted sacraments or established laws and produced customs.

Malinowski further maintained that it was not a case of a leap from the state of nature into that of culture. The earliest elements of culture, namely speech, tradition, material inventions, conceptual thought, came about very slowly. Very small steps accumulated until something we can recognize as culture was produced. Malinowski sums up his analysis thus:

. . . we have found that the totemic crime must have been placed at the very origins of culture; that it must be made the first cause of culture if it is to have any sense at all. This means that we have to assume the crime and its consequences as happening still in the state of nature, but such an assumption involves us in a number of contradictions. We find that there is in reality a complete absence of motive for a parricidal crime, since the working of instincts is in animal conditions well adjusted to the situation; since it leads to conflicts but not to repressed mental states; since concretely the sons have no reason for hating their father after they have left the horde. In the second place we have seen that in the state of nature there is also a complete absence of any means by which the consequences of the totemic crime could have been fixed into the cultural institutions. There is a complete absence of any cultural medium in which ritual, laws, and morals could have been embodied.[28]

Malinowski finally deals with the historical aspects of the supposed crime. How could it have taken place? Are we to suppose that once upon a time and in one super-horde one crime was committed? Or were there many similar or lesser crimes? Are we to suppose that this crime, or crimes, created culture which then spread over the world by diffusion, possibly changing apes into men wherever it reached? Malinowski came to the conclusion that Professor A. L. Kroeber was correct in calling Freud's theory of the primal horde a "Just-so story".

Kroeber returned to this subject again in his *Anthropology* (1948) and his conclusions there can be accepted as those held by competent anthropologists to-day the world over almost without exception:

The psychoanalytic explanation of culture is intuitive, dogmatic, and wholly unhistorical. It disregards the findings of prehistory and archaeology as irrelevant, or at most as dealing only with details of little significance as compared with its own interpretation of the essence of how culture came to be. . . . It is not altogether clear whether the 'event' was construed by Freud in its ordinary sense of a single actual happening, or as a 'typical' recurrent event. But the explanation comes to nearly the same thing in either case; one mechanism is seized upon as cardinal, all evidence of others is disregarded as inconsequential. The theory is obviously as arbitrary as it is fantastically one-sided. It is mentioned only because it is the one *specific* explanation of the culture that has emanated from a psychological source; although Freud was not only far from being orthodox as a psychologist, but treated the findings of psychology almost as highhandedly as he did those of pre-history and culture history.[29]

A small number of psychoanalysts who have turned to anthropology, of whom Géza Róheim is typical, have attempted to give Freud some support. It is probably not an exaggeration to say that Róheim is looked upon more as an advocate of psychoanalysis than as an anthropologist. He began his anthropological work as a convinced and practising psychoanalyst. In 1925 he published his *Australian Totemism* which was a literary and not a field study. From the end of 1928 to the spring of 1931, a short period, Róheim carried out field work in Somaliland, Central Australia, Normanby Island, and among the Yuma Indians of Arizona. During this rapid survey he claims to have found some of the evidence that he was searching for but, follower of Freud though he was, he could not support the whole of the Freudian primal horde hypothesis. In his contribution on "Psychoanalysis and Anthropology" in *Psychoanalysis To-day* (1948) his conclusion was: "From the theoretical point of view the result was that I substituted the ontogenetic theory of culture for the primal horde theory of Freud. Freud believes that in primeval times human beings lived in a form of social organization that has been called the Cyclopean family by Atkinson. . . . Now, I still believe Freud was right in his assumption and that human beings probably lived in groups like the Primal Horde of Freud's *Totem and Taboo*. But what I find unnecessary is the daring hypothesis of a racial unconscious and instead I attempt to base our understanding of human nature on *man's delayed infancy*."[30] Thus even among the most faithful Freudian disciples the original theory was not fully accepted and it had, therefore, to be modified in certain directions.

We can understand why Róheim felt unable to accept the particular form of Freud's "daring hypothesis" of a racial

unconscious as an explanation of the lasting results of the primal
crime, but his own theory about "man's delayed infancy" is not
a satisfactory explanation either. Even if there were evidence—
and there is none—that men lived together in a type of primal
horde, and that the sons combined to kill the father, in what
manner could this deed create the permanent after-effects which
Freud postulated? There is not the slightest evidence for this type
of racial memory, and Freud's hypothesis of a racial unconscious
which could preserve the effects of the original parricide or
parricides appears to have been designed in order to sustain his
vision of the primal deed and its results.

If, then, there is no solid ground for Freud's assumed theory
of the primal horde and the primaeval slaying of the father, his
views of totem and taboo are strongly suspect, for they are
based on these very assumptions.

VI

In totemism the two main taboo prohibitions were (a) not
to kill the totem animal and (b) not to have sexual relations with
any woman of the same totem clan. This corresponded, Freud
maintained, with the kind of social contract made by the brothers
after they had killed the father of the horde, and that is the reason
why the totem animal is not eaten. The taboo on sexual relations
with women of the same totem clan was a repetition of the contract to refrain from sexual intercourse with the wives of the
father. The original deed was responsible for the dread of incest
which is even stronger among primitive peoples than among
civilized races. Freud pointed out Frazer's emphasis on the fact
that the members of a tribe assume the name of their totem, and
also as a rule believe that they are descended from it. Because of
this belief they "do not hunt the totem animal or kill or eat it".[31]
In other words the totem is a father substitute, and is related by
Freud in all its manifestations to the happenings in the primal
horde. If further proof is required, Freud believed that it could
be found in the infantile recurrence of totemism which has been

mentioned at the beginning of this chapter and which is the subject matter of Chapter 4 of *Totem and Taboo*.

Freud's convictions about the existence and nature of the primal horde, the slaying of the father and the taboos which spring from this, appear to have their source in his views about the rôle of the father, whom he regarded as the dominant and sexually jealous male. The sons were, therefore, potential rivals and feared castration by their father: "In the Oedipus as well as in the castration complex the father plays the same rôle of feared opponent to the infantile sexual interests. Castration and its substitute through blinding are the punishment he threatens."[32] Are such impulses always found? Are they, in other words, inevitable parts and, as Freud claimed, the most important and elemental parts of the father's nature?

VII

Malinowski, in *Sex and Repression in Savage Society* to which we have already referred, studied these questions among matrilineal societies in certain island communities in north-western Melanesia. He wished to compare these with the patrilineal family of modern civilization. In these two types of family organization we have the most radically different kinds of family which are known. The Trobriand Islanders are matrilineal. In their social order kinship is reckoned through the mother only, and succession and inheritance descend in the female line. This, in practice, means that the children belong to the mother's family and also to her clan and community. In addition to this the boy succeeds to the dignities and social position of his mother's brother. The boy does not succeed to his father's possessions but to those of his maternal uncle or maternal aunt.

The children are very free in childhood especially in relation to sex. There is a period of sexual play in childhood which is followed by the utmost freedom in adolescence in this respect. Later still, lovers live together in a more permanent relationship. This is followed by matrimony, which is usually monogamous

E

excepting as far as the chiefs are concerned since they have several wives. The marriage is a permanent union and involves sexual exclusion and a common economic existence. This last state might appear superficially to amount to the same pattern of marriage as we find among ourselves. The reality, however, is very different. The husband is not looked upon as the father of the children. Malinowski believed that the natives are ignorant of physical fatherhood and so do not realize that the father is connected physiologically with their birth. The theory is that the children are inserted into the mother's womb as tiny spirits by the spirit of some deceased kinswoman of the mother. The husband, however, has the duty of looking after the children; in fact he usually becomes a very much loved friend. His status with the children is dependent on the nature of his personal relations with them. As far as authority is concerned, that belongs to the mother's brother. The relationship is complicated by the firm taboo which forbids friendly relations between brothers and sisters. The uncle, therefore, can never be intimate with the mother or have access to the household. In practice, the mother recognizes his authority but there is no display of affection between them. As far as the uncle is concerned, his nephews and his nieces are his only heirs and successors and are extremely important to him. They will receive his wealth after his death and even during his life he must pass on to them any special accomplishment which he may possess such as dances, songs, myths, magic and crafts. In addition he supplies his sister and her household with food. All this amounts to the uncle standing for the principles of discipline and authority. The father is looked to for tenderness and is usually regarded as a friend.

The wife has her own possessions and is not at all servile to her husband. He must, of course, work for his own sisters and their children. The father, however, is influential in one respect, for his wife comes to live in his house and community. There is a further matter in which the father has his own sphere of influence because he and the mother are concerned with the marriage of their daughter and, in fact, it is the husband who has authority in this all-important question of his daughter's marriage. This is not an inconsistency but is part of the taboo on the uncle having close personal relations with his sister, and thereby his nieces. Indeed the uncle is forbidden to deal with any sexual matters at all.

Malinowski concludes that in our patrilineal European society we can quite understand the occurrence of the Oedipus complex. Western society influences man's biological nature in a very different way from the matrilineal society of the Trobriand Islanders. In Europe our patriarchal society forms in early childhood a very different system of attitudes which contain elements of hate and also of suppressed desire. There is the influence of the father to prevent a too passionate attachment of the son to the mother. There is, furthermore, the influence of Western morality which condemns expressions of sexuality in children. There is also a clash of social interests between the father and the child. Often the child interferes with the freedom of its parents, and in addition is a reminder of age with its inevitable decline. Therefore, we have all these forces and many others frequently producing—or, if the findings of psychoanalysts are to be accepted, always producing—in our society the familiar phenomena associated with the Oedipus complex.

Although these forces and influences are not to be found in the matrilineal society of the Trobriand Islander, other repressing forces do exist, and Malinowski points out that they are twofold. First there is the submission to the matriarchal tribal law, and secondly the prohibitions of exogamy. The submission to the matriarchal tribal law is brought about by the authority of the mother's brother. The relationship with this uncle is influenced both by the demands which he makes and the inevitable rivalry between the successor and the succeeded, and so jealousy and resentment are found as typical parts of the relationship between uncle and nephew. There is something of an ambivalent attitude in the relationship, in which consciously admiration would appear to be dominant but actually there is also present a repressed hatred. A second taboo is contained in the prohibitions of incest. This refers to the sister, and also to a lesser degree to other family

relatives on the mother's side, as well as to women who belong
to that particular clan. Undoubtedly, however, the taboo relates
most strongly to the sister and is so strong that it prevents much
tenderness towards her.

In the patriarchal society we find that the early rivalries and
the later social functions complicate the attitude of father and son,
until we find a certain measure of attachment but, at the same
time, resentment and dislike. But as far as the mother and son
are concerned, very early separation in infancy leaves an un-
satisfied craving which later becomes connected with the growing
sensual interest, and frequently takes on a neurotic character
which is revealed in dreams and other fantasies. Among the
Trobriands, where there is no such friction between the father
and son, the child's craving for its mother is expressed simply
and spontaneously. The result is that the ambivalent attitude of
admiration or veneration and dislike is expressed between a man
and his maternal uncle, and the repressed sexual attitude of
incestuous temptation manifests itself towards his sister. Malinowski stated: "Applying to each society a terse, though somewhat
crude formula, we might say that in the Oedipus complex
there is the repressed desire to kill the father and marry the
mother, while in the matrilineal society of the Trobriands the
wish is to marry the sister and to kill the maternal uncle."[33]

He goes on to suggest that this situation indicates a hatred
of authority and is not inspired by sexual jealousy, for the sons
are aware that it is the father who has sexual intercourse with the
mother and not the uncle. This is true even if Malinowski was
correct, which he probably was not, in thinking that the Trobriand Islanders were ignorant of the connection between
parenthood and sexual intercourse.

VIII

Freud assumed that he was well acquainted with all the impulses which are present in the human family. Malinowski's
work revealed that this was not so. At the most Freud could

speak for one type of family, the typical western European family
of the late nineteenth and early twentieth centuries. Even there
he stressed some of the elements and missed others. And even
if the primal horde had been found at any time, and it has not
been, there is no reason to think that it would fully substantiate
Freudian theories about the rôle of the father. There are other
possible interpretations of the phenomena with which Freud
dealt. Fromm, for instance, in discussing Freud's view that the
Oedipus complex is the core of every neurosis, suggests that we
should learn more if we understood that what Freud called incest
was not in reality a sexual craving for members of the same
family, but "one expression of the much more profound and
fundamental desire to remain a child attached to those protecting
figures of whom the mother is the earliest and most influential".[34]

What Freud considered to be the place of the father in the
Oedipus complex, which he had constantly encountered in his
analytical work, was fundamental to his theory of totemism.
But just how selective he was in his treatment of totemism is
shown very clearly by the researches in this subject by Goldenweiser, published in the *Journal of American Folklore* in 1910, two
years before *Totem and Taboo* was published. If only he had
studied Goldenweiser's work he could not have made the generalizations which he did. In Goldenweiser's thesis he would have
found ample evidence for the following statements:

> Exogamy, taboo, religious regard, totemic names, descent from
> the totem—all fail as invariable characteristics of totemism.
> Each of these traits, moreover, displays more or less striking
> independence in its distribution; and most of them can be
> shown to be widely-spread ethnic phenomena, diverse in
> origin, not necessarily co-ordinated in development, and
> displaying a rich variability of psychological make-up.
>
> If we must regard the groups of phenomena which in
> various areas have been termed 'totemic' as conglomerates of
> essentially independent features, the fundamental error in two
> lines of totemistic inquiry and speculation becomes at once

apparent. I mean the attempts to assign to the various factors in totemism a correlated historical development, and the tendency to either combine these factors or derive them from each other, psychologically. An integral development of totemism loses its plausibility, in view of the demonstrated historical independence of its factors; while the psychological complexity and variability of the latter discourages any attempt at direct psychological derivations. Either one of the factors could with equal plausibility be taken as a starting-point, and the others could be derived from it without transgressing the bounds of either historical or psychological possibilities. The interpretative value, however, of such derivations, as well as of similar ones actually attempted, is *nil*.[35]

It is easy to speculate about the origin of exogamy (or endogamy) on general sociological, psychological, or physiological grounds. Any number of possible developments may be guessed at, and in a given case several may seem plausible or even probable; but in the absence of an historic backbone, the interpretative value of such speculations is *nil*.[36]

As most present-day anthropologists support Goldenweiser's contention that it is impossible to discover invariable characteristics of totemism, we can understand that totemism itself is not easy to define, especially as the term has often been used to cover any beliefs or practices related to some supposed connection between animals or other natural phenomena, and persons. In most groups the totem animal must not be killed or eaten, but in a small number of groups it can be. And the totem feast which has a large place in Freud's theories in *Totem and Taboo* is extremely rare.

IX

We need a more comprehensive view of totemism than that given by Freud, for totemism deals with the general relations between certain groups and some definite objects or phenomena, and these relations tend to have mythological and ritual aspects. Freud did not allow for the fact that what he regarded as the special features of totemism are not all inherently totemic in themselves, but occur as customs apart from totemism. For instance, exogamy is usually found along with totemism but is not necessarily vitally connected with it, for some form of exogamy is found in all human societies. Totemic exogamy is the natural outcome of a society organized in totemic clans or groups.

Speculations about the origin of totemism are valueless as they are incapable of verification. Many theories about its nature exist apart from that put forward by Freud. One is that it is connected with taboos on the destruction of creatures and objects of economic value, another that it is related to trade and exchange practices. It has also been regarded as an outgrowth of primitive ideas about sexual conception. Yet another theory has seen its main significance as an expression of individual guardian spirits.

Freud's theories are clearly inadequate and they make totemism almost meaningless to those who practise it. There is a deeper meaning in much of totemism which Freud missed. A. P. Elkin in his *The Australian Aborigines* says: "Totemism is more than a mechanism for regulating marriage. It is a view of nature and life, of the universe and man, which colours and influences the Aborigines' social groupings and mythologies, inspires their rituals and links them to the past."[37]

Elkin also stresses the variety of forms in totemism which makes it so very complex. Each person in a tribe may have three or four totems or, to put it in another way, may belong to that number of totemic groups. "But this is only the beginning of the complexity, for as we shall see, on the one hand, one form may have more than one function and on the other hand, several forms perform a similar function. It is, therefore, necessary to study totemic phenomena from the point of view of the function which they perform in social and religious life."[38] Totemism expresses a view of nature and life and the manner in which the totemite is related to it, and so it may be regarded as the precursor of philosophy.

In a section on "The Totemic View of Life" Elkin maintains that the theme of totemism is that man and natural species are brought into one social and ceremonial whole, sharing a common life. In social totemism the totem has the twofold function of symbolizing the common relationship of members of the human group and also acting as their friend or guardian; the group on their part respect it and would not injure it unless there were an absolute necessity to do so. In cult totemism the totem is an emblem or hero commemorated by the members, but it is also the life of the species and they are ritually responsible for its increase. Basically this symbolism rests on the conviction that man and nature belong to one order. The ritual for the increase of the species does not attempt to control nature by magical means but is a method of expressing man's needs, especially his need for the normal order of nature to be maintained. Fundamentally it is bound up with a system of co-operation with nature which has both economic and psychological functions in that it expresses economic facts and needs and, in addition, gives confidence in the processes of nature and hope for the future.

Elkin shows that individual and assistant totemism is also based on the central tenet of totemism that men and natural species share in a common life. It is taken for granted that man and his totem are in personal and intimate contact and that the totem can come to the man's aid. The totem has a similar function in dreams, where it symbolizes the totemite and serves him by bringing information and in other ways. This proves that totemism is a form of animism, for the totems are endowed with spirits or personalities.

The principle of the unity of man and nature is clearly and interestingly expressed through classificatory totemism. What this amounts to is a division and classification of men and indeed of all natural phenomena which are in any way of interest to man in one system. Thus in effect there is no separation of human beings from natural species and objects.

The moiety, clan and other groups include, in addition to a number of men and women, certain natural species and objects.

Aborigines can usually indicate at once to which moiety or other group such objects as the kangaroo, the bamboo, grasses or stones belong; in fact they are as familiar with this as with the moiety, clan or section of their fellow-clansmen. The classification is based on the relationship between human beings, natural species and phenomena which the native takes for granted as existing and which, therefore, he groups together.

The moieties [writes Elkin] are always associated with other subdivisions, namely clans or sections: in all tribes in which totemism is a means of expressing the unity of man and nature as 'one big tribe', men and women and all things are classified not only between the moieties, but also between the clans or sections. In such case, we speak of multiple totemism and of sub-totems or subsidiary totems. For example, the clan totem may be kangaroo; it is therefore the totem of a human group, and, in addition, of a group of natural objects and species. Thus grass, water, the Pleiades and so on are kangaroo, just as are certain men and women. To the latter, kangaroo is the primary totem, while grass, water, the Pleiades etc., are subsidiary totems; but though they are only secondary, they are objects of respect and can be expected to serve (warn and help) the members of the human kangaroo clan.[39]

In Australia totemism is so much a part of man's being that it has its place in all his social and ritual groupings. It expresses the common life and mutual dependence which man and nature share. "The result is that whatever be his form of social grouping, he must bring the whole of nature into it, for just as there can be no loose human remnants—that is, individuals—without clan or section, so also there can be nothing in heaven or earth in such a predicament."[40] Thus man feels at home with nature because all species, objects and phenomena are brought into his social system and are made part of his own kinship, moiety, clan or other organization. He can, therefore, deal with it in the same manner as the various groups of his fellow-men. In this way nature is humanized if not personified and we approach, and possibly find, a spiritual and animistic view of the universe.

Freud's view of totemism is in a different world from that of Elkin. Freud looks back to a hypothetical cause—the slaying of the primal father—and its effects. Totemism is a dying survival and its heir, the Oedipus complex, is already in possession among most men. Elkin finds none of this and for him totemism has its roots in a primitive view of life, and the way in which primitive man thinks of himself as related to the rest of the universe. It is a real force in the present not because of some vague racial memory of some primal far-off event, but because it is the system which gives meaning to all his relationships, human and otherwise. It is the way in which he sees and feels his world.

A similar view is expressed by A. R. Radcliffe-Brown in his *Structure and Function in Primitive Society*:

> It will be part of my thesis in this paper that however widely or narrowly we may define totemism, we cannot reach an understanding of the phenomena we so name unless we study systematically a much wider group of phenomena, namely, the general relation between man and natural species in mythology and ritual. It may well be asked if 'totemism' as a technical term has not outlived its usefulness.[41]

He also writes:

> Although there is always a danger in short formulas I think it does not misrepresent Australian totemism to describe it as a mechanism by which a system of social solidarities is established between man and nature. The mechanism has been worked out in many different ways, and much more elaborately in some than in others, but everywhere it possesses this character.
>
> The suggestion I put forward, therefore, is that totemism is part of a larger whole, and that one important way in which we can characterize this whole is that it provides a representation of the universe as a moral or social order.[42]

Freud's view of totemism, therefore, cannot be accepted. He concentrated on its origins or causes and was, moreover, convinced on theoretical grounds that he had the key to the understanding of these. Few anthropologists can be better acquainted with all the problems connected with such a quest than Radcliffe-Brown, and his views on this subject are as follows:

In the past the theoretical discussion of totemism was almost entirely concerned with speculations as to its possible origin. If we use the word origin to mean the historical process by which an institution or custom or a state of culture comes into existence, then it is clear that the very diverse forms of totemism that exist all over the world must have had very diverse origins. To be able to speak of an origin of totemism we must assume that all these diverse institutions that we include under the one general term have been derived by successive modifications from a single form. There does not seem to me to be a particle of evidence to justify such an assumption. But even if we make it we can still only speculate as to what this original form of totemism may have been, as to the enormously complex series of events which could have produced from it the various existing totemic systems, and as to where, when, and how that hypothetical original form of totemism came into existence. And such speculations, being for ever incapable of inductive verification, can be nothing more than speculations and can have no value for a science of culture.[43]

X

Was Freud, then, more convincing in his treatment of taboo than he was of totemism? He was confident that he could solve all the problems connected with this subject for he claims in his preface to *Totem and Taboo*, "The problem of taboo is presented more exhaustively, and the effort to solve it is approached with perfect confidence".[44]

He examined taboos in relation to (*a*) the treatment of enemies, (*b*) rulers and (*c*) the dead, and maintained that an ambivalent attitude is present towards the object of a taboo. The unconscious would like nothing better than to transgress the taboo for "The basis of taboo is a forbidden action for which there exists a strong inclination in the unconscious",[45] but people "are afraid just because they would like to transgress, and the fear is stronger than the pleasure".[46] So a taboo derives its power, its reality, through the presence of both desire and fear. Love and hate can exist towards the same object, as Freud illustrated from his experience with neurotics. He also maintained "that the psychic impulses of primitive man possessed a higher degree of ambivalence than is found at present among civilized human beings. With the decline of this ambivalence the taboo, as the compromise symptom of the ambivalent conflict, also slowly disappeared."[47]

Unfortunately, Freud did not deal with the wider implications of the taboos which he lists in the treatment of enemies, rulers, and the dead, but concentrated on "the oldest and most important taboo prohibitions [which] are the two basic laws of totemism: namely not to kill the totem animal, and to avoid sexual intercourse with totem companions of the other sex. It would therefore seem that these must have been the oldest and strongest desires of mankind."[48] Freud's statement that these were the oldest taboo prohibitions once again meant an assumption about origins where no direct evidence was available. He would also have done well to examine the question as to why he called them the "most important taboo prohibitions". It appears as if the answer was that they were important from the standpoint of his own theories, for this was exactly the use he made of them: "If the totem animal is the father," (and this was the conclusion to which he had come) "then the two main commandments of totemism, the two taboo rules which constitute its nucleus—not to kill the totem animal and not to use a woman belonging to the same totem for sexual purposes—agree in content with the two crimes of Oedipus, who slew his father and took his mother to wife, and also with the child's two primal wishes whose insufficient repression or whose reawakening forms the nucleus of perhaps all neuroses."[49]

XI

As with totemism then so with taboo, there is a narrowing of interest until it is concentrated on what appears to fit in with psychoanalytical theory. The result is a presentation of taboo which is far too narrow to cover the wide range of its phenomena. The contribution of Raymond Firth's book, *Primitive Economics of the New Zealand Maori*, on this subject is notable and relevant. Professor Firth deals with one important aspect which was frequently present although neglected by Freud, and he also discusses the Freudian theories of taboo.

In a section on *tapu* (taboo) Firth indicates its importance in economic life where it was concerned with natural resources, highly valued cultural objects, and man himself. It protected trees and other property of value. Important natural resources like food and anything economically essential were respected because it was believed that *tapu* resided in them. In practice *tapu* implied a recognition of the social value of such objects as canoes and superior houses. Men themselves were also protected by their personal *tapu* and the amount which they possessed increased with their rank. So *tapu* protected private property such as food, fish and forests, and was a source of order restraining the naturally warlike and turbulent Maori and making him obedient, orderly and law-abiding.

An analysis of the institution of *tapu* in its economic aspect shows then that it has distinct practical effects. It expresses the recognition of the 'social value' of things to man, of their importance in his scheme of existence. It provides also a valuable system for the regulation of conduct; it sacralizes and sets apart things with which the ordinary individual should not meddle, and by the associated belief in supernatural punishment for infringement imposes a religious sanction upon these rules. Moreover, in the production of the more important economic goods the *tapu* often imposes an adherence to work and a concentration of energy which are of the utmost value.[50]

Firth discusses Freud's theories as given in *Totem and Taboo* and states that for Freud the taboo restrictions are different from religious or moral prohibitions in that they have an arbitrary nature. The prohibitions of taboo, for Freud, are the analogue of individual compulsion neurosis. The sources of taboo are ambivalent emotional attitudes in which social components have largely replaced the sexual elements of the neurosis. Undoubtedly emotional factors are a part of taboo, but Freud does not allow sufficiently for other factors. Taboo regulations possess a social as well as an individual character. More than this, the taboos in a society "form an organized, integrated system, each prohibition having its place in the great scheme of traditional belief".[51] The compulsion neurotic's 'taboos' are arbitrary and peculiar to himself and although they may be a part of his organized system of belief they have no meaning for society in general. At this point there is no correspondence between taboo and the phenomena connected with compulsion neurosis. Freud fails to convince because he attempts to explain taboo too much in terms of individual psychology.

Firth believes that for these reasons the effort to find the roots of taboo in unconscious forbidden desires unduly strains the evidence. It is clear that the wish to break through prohibitions is often present, but quite consciously, as for instance towards the taboo placed on food supplies. Further, Freud neglects the positive aspects of taboo regulations. Their function is not always to prohibit, for they often enforce certain courses of action. The taboo of net-making calls for work, but "the desire to violate the taboo", which would be to stop work, is consciously present. Some taboos demand abstinence from sexual intercourse, but the wish to break this taboo is often a conscious one.

Firth concludes: "The *tapu* must always be studied as an institution working in the community, not as an aggregate of isolated individual prohibitions . . . its essence is seen to consist in a standardization through tradition of valuable emotional attitudes largely of conscious kind towards objects of cultural importance."[52] The *tapu* could be removed by special ceremonies.

Goldenweiser in his *Anthropology* endorses Firth's views and gives further support to a far wider application of taboo than Freud ever implied:

In the economic life and ideas of the Maori the influence of taboo was all-pervasive. Forests were under the guardianship of the god Tane, who protected the trees, rats, birds, and all woodland products from unauthorized interference.

The concept and nature of taboo, as operative among the Maori, is best understood by associating it with the correlated notion of a non-material core or 'life principle' (*mauri*) which was connected with all things in nature and gave them their vitality, in fact their very existence. In the case of a forest, for example, its fertility and productive power depended upon its *mauri*. The fruiting of trees, the abundance of birds and rats, all hinged upon the preservation of their *mauri* intact. The same applied to fisheries. Firth correctly notes that this *mauri* was an intangible and imponderable essence, impersonal in character. It should not be confused with the notion of an indwelling spirit. In the various economic undertakings of their daily life the Maori, while using the resources provided by their environment, were careful not to interfere with the *mauri* of these things, thus contaminating them. Hence the taboo regulations.[53]

XII

We have had to discuss Freud's theories on totem and taboo at length, and also his 'visions' of all that resulted from the primal horde, for these were the foundations for the conclusions he drew about the nature of religion. At first sight *Totem and Taboo* appears to be chiefly a study of these subjects, but in *An Autobiographical Study* Freud himself makes clear the high value he set on his contributions to the psychology of religion, and he mentions this book, *Totem and Taboo*, more than any other. His conclusions have been given at the beginning of this chapter. Because of their definite nature it appeared at first that we should have to devote a considerable amount of space to a discussion of the implications arising from these conclusions. But clearly their value entirely depends on the value of his main theories about the primal horde and totem and taboo. If these cannot be accepted as reliable, then what Freud has to say about religion does not follow and, indeed, there is almost nothing to discuss. We are not in fact dealing with the experiences of religion, but with what Freud imagined religious experience to be.

He makes the sweeping and irrelevant statement at the end of *Totem and Taboo*: "In the beginning was the deed". The truth is that neither he nor anyone else can be sure of what there was in the beginning. His presentation of totem and taboo, carefully selected to fit the theory he accepted of the primal horde in particular and psychoanalysis in general, is completely inadequate and unconvincing. By over-simplification it avoids the complexity of these vast subjects and their widespread significance covering the whole of life among their adherents.

In *Totem and Taboo* Freud treated religion as a by-product of the situation he described. It is a fairy story, but if we believe his version of the origins of religion to be a fairy story, it follows that his basis for calling religion one has gone, and there is nothing in his argument left to answer.

NOTES TO CHAPTER 3

[1] S. Freud, *An Autobiographical Study*, trans. James Strachey. London, Hogarth Press (1935), p. 121.

[2] *Ibid.*, p. 121.

[3] *Ibid.*, p. 122.

[4] S. Freud, *Totem and Taboo*, trans. A. A. Brill. London, Pelican Books edn. (1938), p. 17.

[5] S. Freud, *An Autobiographical Study*, p. 123.

[6] *Ibid.*, p. 123.

[7] *Ibid.*, p. 123.

[8] *Ibid.*, p. 123.

[9] *Ibid.*, pp. 123-4.

[10] *Ibid.*, p. 124.

[11] *Ibid.*, pp. 124-5.

[12] *Ibid.*, p. 125.

[13] *Ibid.*, p. 126.

[14] *Ibid.*, p. 126.

[15] *Ibid.*, p. 126.
[16] S. Freud, *Totem and Taboo*, p. 138.
[17] *Ibid.*, p. 196.
[18] *Ibid.*, p. 196.
[19] *Ibid.*, pp. 204-5.
[20] *Ibid.*, p. 205.
[21] *Ibid.*, p. 205.
[22] *Ibid.*, p. 213.
[23] *Ibid.*, p. 207.
[24] *Ibid.*, p. 189.
[25] S. Freud, *An Autobiographical Study*, p. 125.
[26] *Ibid.*, pp. 122-3.
[27] B. Malinowski, *Sex and Repression in Savage Society*. London, Kegan Paul (1927), p. 155.
[28] *Ibid.*, pp. 166-7.
[29] A. L. Kroeber, *Anthropology*, revised edn. New York, Harcourt, Brace & Co. (1948), pp. 616-17.
[30] G. Róheim, "Psychoanalysis and Anthropology" in *Psycho-analysis Today*, edited by Sandor Lorand. London, Allen & Unwin (1948), p. 383.
[31] S. Freud, *Totem and Taboo*, p. 143.
[32] *Ibid.*, p. 175.
[33] B. Malinowski, *op. cit.*, pp. 80-1.
[34] Erich Fromm, *Psychoanalysis and Religion*. London, Gollancz (1951), p. 85.
[35] A. A. Goldenweiser, "Totemism and Analytical Study", *Journal of American Folklore*, vol. XXIII, 179-293 (1910), p. 266.
[36] *Ibid.*, p. 247 n.
[37] A. P. Elkin, *The Australian Aborigines*. Sydney, Angus & Robertson (1938), p. 126.
[38] *Ibid.*, p. 133.
[39] *Ibid.*, pp. 184-5.
[40] *Ibid.*, p. 185.
[41] A. R. Radcliffe-Brown, *Structure and Function in Primitive Society*. London, Cohen & West (1952), p. 117.
[42] *Ibid.*, p. 131.
[43] *Ibid.*, p. 122.
[44] S. Freud, *Totem and Taboo*, p. 6.
[45] *Ibid.*, p. 54.
[46] *Ibid.*, p. 54.
[47] *Ibid.*, pp. 96-7.
[48] *Ibid.*, p. 54.
[49] *Ibid.*, pp. 177-8.
[50] R. Firth, *Primitive Economics of the New Zealand Maori*. London, George Routledge & Sons (1929), p. 238.
[51] *Ibid.*, p. 240.
[52] *Ibid.*, p. 241.
[53] A. A. Goldenweiser, *Anthropology*. New York, Appleton-Century-Crofts, 1937 (1946 printing), pp. 235-6.

F

4

The Future of an Illusion

"No, science is no illusion. But it would be an illusion to suppose
that we could get anywhere else what it cannot give us."
SIGMUND FREUD, *The Future of an Illusion* (p. 98).

I

IN 1927 Freud, in *The Future of an Illusion*, made his strongest
attack on religion. The illusion, of course, was religion, and his
thesis: that it had no future. In this book there is no closely
argued theme and nothing factual. Freud was seventy-one when
he wrote it and it reads like the statement of the beliefs of a
disillusioned old man, although there can be nothing but admiration for his courage and honesty. The book deals with three main
subjects, culture, religion and science.

Freud based what he had to say about culture on his assumptions about the social nature of man. In this book even the
findings of psychoanalysis do not play a large part. We have
Freud's assumptions, prejudices and views, and they appear to
reflect his constitutional pessimism, his convinced atheism un-
examined since adolescence, and above all his fearless honesty.
His statements throw more light on his own nature than on his
subject matter, and although he makes many pronouncements
his views are commonplace.

What, for example, is the source of his statement on p. 9:
"The mutual relations of men are profoundly influenced by the
measure of instinctual satisfaction that the existing resources
make possible; secondly, because the individual can himself take
on the quality of a piece of property in relation to another, in
so far as this other makes use of his capacity for work or chooses

68

him as sexual object; and thirdly, because every individual is virtually an enemy of culture, which is nevertheless ostensibly an object of universal human concern"?

He produced no proof, or even argument, for his assumption that every individual is virtually an enemy of culture, although that is clearly expressed as his view of human nature. He also assumed that this tendency in the individual is so powerful that it is impossible to do without a government of the masses by a minority: "The masses are lazy and unintelligent, they have no love for instinctual renunciation, they are not to be convinced of its inevitability by argument, and the individuals support each other in giving full play to their unruliness."[1] Some individuals must set an example so that the masses can recognize their leaders, and Freud carried the leadership principle so far as to say: "Therefore it seems necessary that they [the leaders] should be independent of the masses by having at their disposal means of enforcing their authority."[2] He could see something of the implications of this doctrine, for on p. 15 he referred to the great cultural experiment which at that very time was taking place in Russia and wrote: "I have neither the special knowledge nor the capacity to decide on its practicability, to test the expediency of the methods employed, or to measure the width of the inevitable gulf between intention and execution." It is dangerous to suspend judgment too long about the necessity for democracy. It is dangerous to despise the masses and it is still more perilous to maintain that the masses must be governed by a minority of leaders who will be independent of them and possess the means of enforcing their authority. How dangerous, how perilous Freud learnt during the bitter years of the Nazis' rule when they put into practice the mastery of the masses by their own dedicated minority.

For Freud culture was extremely unstable because the pressure it exercises and the instinctual renunciations it demands create constant hostility towards it. He stated his view of man's true desires and saw in them a reason for a continual conflict with society: "If one imagined its prohibitions removed, then one could choose any woman who took one's fancy as one's sexual object, one could kill without hesitation one's rival or whoever interfered with one in any other way, and one could seize what one wanted of another man's goods without asking his leave: how splendid, what a succession of delights, life would be!"[3]

He continued by asserting that culture is essential, and that its real function is the preservation of mankind against the supremacy of nature, for nature is still largely untamed. The earth quakes, is rent asunder and man with all his works is buried. Man can be the victim of tumult and flood and also of various diseases. Finally, there is the painful riddle of death for which no remedy at all has yet been found, nor probably ever will be. So nature rises before us "sublime, pitiless, inexorable", reminding us of our weakness and helplessness.

II

When man faces all these forces of nature he finds that there is nothing new in the situation for it is similar to what he has experienced as a child. He knew then a condition of helplessness, but the place of nature was taken by parents. The child feared his parents, especially the father, but at the same time knew that he was a protection against possible dangers. As a result of this infantile experience Freud argued that man endues the forces of nature with the characteristics of the father and makes them into gods. Even when man observes traces of law and order in natural phenomena his helplessness remains, and with it his longing for the all-powerful father and the gods, and the latter retain their threefold task:

1. They must exorcise the terrors of nature.
2. They must reconcile the individual to the cruelty of fate, particularly as shown in death.
3. They must make amends for the sufferings and privations that the communal life of culture has imposed on man.

THE FUTURE OF AN ILLUSION

Freud repeated this theme and expressed it still more simply: "I have tried to show that religious ideas have sprung from the same need as all the other achievements of culture: from the necessity for defending itself against the crushing supremacy of nature. And there was a second motive: the eager desire to correct the so painfully felt imperfections of culture."[4] The father-god is created by man's need for defence because of human weakness. Freud maintained that it is natural for man, following an infantile prototype, to project his experiences and to look upon all events outside himself as owing their existence to beings who are fundamentally like himself, and in this way he personifies the forces of nature.

Freud admitted that the psychological significance of religious ideas and their classification are not easy to give, and then defined religion to prepare the way for this task: "religion consists of certain dogmas, assertions about facts and conditions of external (or internal) reality, which tell one something that one has not oneself discovered and which claim that one should give them credence."[5] It is a narrow definition which allows no place for individual religious experience or for the possibility that the formulated dogmas may be completely inadequate to deal with the richness of the religious experiences which created them. Indeed many people, including mystics, would claim that their experiences cannot be expressed clearly in terms of dogma. Freud, however, assumed that his definition covered everything, and goes on to state: "If all the arguments that are put forward for the authenticity of religious doctrines originate in the past, it is natural to look round and see whether the present, better able to judge in these matters, cannot also furnish such evidence."[6]

The kind of evidence which Freud required is revealed by the illustration he gives from geography, where a student might be told that Konstanz is on the Bodensee. This can be put to the test and Freud had indeed proved that it was true by going there. The way to personal conviction in such matters is open to test: we can go and see. Freud continued: "Let us try to apply the same tests to the dogmas of religion. If we ask on what their claim to be believed is based, we receive three answers, which accord remarkably ill with one another. They deserve to be believed: firstly, because our primal ancestors already believed them; secondly, because we possess proofs, which have been handed down to us from this very period of antiquity; and thirdly, because it is forbidden to raise the question of their authenticity at all."[7] He did not state where these answers came from but certainly they could not have come from any competent theologian, nor from an intelligent believer. The answers reveal one thing only: the manner in which he himself thought about religion. They were *his* answers and no one else's. If the answers really covered the nature of religion then it would indeed be open to suspicion. But suppose we apply the same tests to some of Freud's psychological beliefs, such as the Oedipus complex or the slaying of the primal father. We cannot go and see the proof as we can in the instance of Konstanz, but this does not mean that Freud is necessarily wrong, for we may be applying a completely inappropriate test. That is exactly what Freud did to the dogmas of religion, and, what was still more serious, his definition of religion clearly shows that he confused the dogmas with religion itself.

We are, as Freud acknowledged, confronted with a fresh psychological problem in that "in spite of their incontrovertible lack of authenticity, religious ideas have exercised the very strongest influence on mankind".[8] We must therefore "ask where the inherent strength of these doctrines lies and to what circumstance they owe their efficacy, independent, as it is, of the acknowledgment of the reason". They are not, Freud said, the residue of experience or the final result of reflection but "they are illusions, fulfilments of the oldest, strongest and most insistent wishes of mankind; the secret of their strength is the strength of these wishes".[9] These wishes proceed from the terrifying effect of infantile helplessness which arouses the need for protection to be sought when possible through the father's love. Later experience leads to the discovery that this feeling of helplessness continues throughout life and so it is necessary for the adult to cling to the existence of an all-powerful father. Man wishes to believe in the benevolent rule of a divine providence which would overcome his anxiety in the face of life's dangers and establish a moral world order which would ensure justice. In addition death would lose its sting, since religion promises a future life. But it is obvious that Freud was holding no independent enquiry into the origin and psychology of religion, for he had made up his mind with absolute finality that it is an illusion in the ordinary sense of the word, that it has an "incontrovertible lack of authenticity", and is independent of reason.

III

His subject was "The Future of an Illusion" and it is, therefore, important to understand exactly what he meant by this word for it carries us to the heart of his argument: "An illusion is not the same as an error, it is indeed not necessarily an error".[10] The characteristic of an illusion is that it is derived from men's wishes, and he gave as an illustration the illusion which a poor girl might have that a prince will come and rescue her, and indeed there is a possibility that this might happen for there have been such cases. When he came to apply it to religious doctrines he appeared to forget his definition that an illusion is derived from men's wishes and is not necessarily an error: "If after this survey we turn again to religious doctrines, we may reiterate that they are all illusions, they do not admit of proof, and no one can be compelled to consider them as true or to believe in them."[11] Later in the same paragraph he revealed his own assumptions very clearly: "The riddles of the universe only reveal themselves slowly to our enquiry, to many questions science can as yet give no answer; but scientific work is our only way to the knowledge of external reality."[12]

IV

If religion is incontrovertibly lacking in authenticity and not influenced by reason, there must surely be some explanation for its survival other than wishes. Freud believed that it is maintained by rationalization: "Where questions of religion are concerned people are guilty of every possible kind of insincerity and intellectual misdemeanour."[13] Even philosophers, he insisted, will stretch the meaning of words. Apparently recognizing the limitations of his psychological investigation of religion he went on: "It does not lie within the scope of this enquiry to estimate the value of religious doctrines as truth. It suffices that we have recognized them, psychologically considered, as illusions,"[14] adding immediately after that this discovery strongly influences our attitude to religion, especially when we bear in mind that it can be known at what periods and by what sort of men religious doctrines were formed, and also the motives which were responsible: "We say to ourselves: it would indeed be very nice if there were a God, who was both creator of the world and a benevolent providence, if there were a moral world order and a future life, but at the same time it is very odd that this is all just as we should wish it ourselves. And it would be still odder if our poor, ignorant, enslaved ancestors had succeeded in solving all these difficult riddles of the universe."[15]

His definition of religion, stressing as it did our belief in certain dogmas because our primal ancestors already believed them, or because of proofs which have been handed down to us from antiquity, or because we have been forbidden to raise the question of their authenticity at all, was not consistent with his other main argument that religion owed its existence to our sense of need. This dry, rational definition is far from the dynamic, god-creating material of our insistent wishes. If these are the forces which make religion, then the definition will have to be different. One cannot condemn religion as a meaningless heritage from the past, claiming that because it has its origins there we can know nothing about it in our personal experience and, at the same time, condemn it on the grounds that it is nothing more than the creation of wish-fulfilment acting in the present: in other words, that we create gods because we cannot face reality. There is a decided inconsistency here. Freud gave two explanations and they do not agree. Convinced that religion is an illusion he argued against it, but all the time from the standpoint of someone entirely outside the experience of religion itself. He projected on to the believer from his own outlook, never realizing how entirely different the experience of the believer is. Allowing for the projections of everyone else, he overlooked his own.

V

The Future of an Illusion was a confession of faith. Religion, Freud insisted, belonged to the past when it had performed some services for human culture, but it had no future, because the future belonged to science. Making the doubtful claim that religion was decreasing in influence because belief had become less universal, he gave as his reason, "the increase of the scientific spirit in the higher strata of human society. Criticism has nibbled at the authenticity of religious documents, natural science has shown up the errors contained in them, and the comparative method of research has revealed the fatal resemblance between religious ideas revered by us and the mental productions of primitive ages and peoples."[16] As the fruits of knowledge became more accessible so, Freud believed, would religious belief steadily decline and this process could not be halted.

VI

Theodor Reik, one of his most faithful disciples, delivered a critical paper (later published in his book *From Thirty Years with Freud*) at one of Freud's famous Wednesday meetings in December, 1927, on *The Future of an Illusion*. As one would expect, Reik found much to praise in Freud's book, saying that in the first part of his essay he thought Freud had imparted knowledge, but in the latter part he had made a confession of faith: "We shall not withhold our great admiration for this brilliantly delineated picture of the future; but it seems to us less compelling than the foregoing. Moreover, it is admittedly more dependent on subjective factors than the rest. It is not outside the bounds of possibility that this picture of Freud's will become reality; but it is certainly striking that his view of the future in the main seems to conform to our wishes. Whereas the main section of Freud's essay shows the future of an illusion, we may say with little exaggeration that this last section presents the illusion of a future."[17]

There is much in *The Future of an Illusion* to suggest that Freud could not do without his particular illusion, for he had his own strong wishes and their fulfilment was related to the progress of science. He was, as we know, a man of his age as far as science was concerned, and it was an optimistic age in this respect. For him the future belonged to the scientist: "Since the time of the deluge science has taught him much, and it will still further increase his power."[18] "We believe that it is possible for scientific work to discover something about the reality of the world through which we can increase our power and according to which we can regulate our life. If this belief is an illusion, then we are in the same position as you, but science has shown us by numerous and significant successes that it is no illusion."[19] His final paragraph is: "No, science is no illusion. But it would be an illusion to suppose that we could get anywhere else what it cannot give us."[20] In the light of later scientific developments in warfare Freud's hopes sound pathetic and naïve. If we still hope for a heaven on earth we no longer expect it to come through science alone.

VII

Freud was exceedingly distrustful of what he called "the oldest, strongest and most insistent wishes of mankind", and very suspicious of "the psychical origins of religious ideas" which he believed had their foundation in these wishes. Anything which owed its existence to wish-fulfilment was suspect, and the term 'wishful thinking', in a derogatory sense, has now come into general use. But he did not make the scope of wish-fulfilment sufficiently clear. At times he appeared to be suspicious of anything remotely connected with wishes, and to regard them as being invariably deceptive. Probably his opinion was that wishes which were in accord with the reality principle could be admitted, but where the pleasure principle operated they were likely to lead only to fantasies. Apparently he disliked wishes for the reason that from their very nature they lead to pleasure, and so are almost certain to be bound up with the pleasure principle. If a wish related to something which could be, and was, tested then it would be in accordance with the reality principle. There are, however, difficulties in this view. There does not, for example, seem to be any intrinsic reason why the productions of the pleasure principle should not also be in accordance with the reality principle. And what is even more difficult is to distinguish reality itself in some realms.

At times we may have one of the oldest and most insistent wishes of mankind, namely the wish for food. If we are hungry this is a perfectly healthy wish and Freud could have shown at once as a doctor that the wish was on correct and natural lines, for our bodies must be nourished and so the wish is in accordance with reality principles. We may have a wish for wealth and much of our daily labour may be inspired by this wish. Once again it could be shown that money is essential to enable us to buy the means of subsistence, and where there is a surplus it could be the means of enlarging and enriching our lives. Here, then, we have another example of a perfectly healthy wish, for it stands up to reality testing. Perhaps we may wish to gain wealth in other ways, and accordingly complete football pool entries every week. If we know the statistical improbabilities of gaining wealth in that manner, and treat the venture accordingly, our attitude may be healthy. If we treat the wish otherwise we are guilty of wishful thinking and the odds of our wishful thinking can be exactly calculated. Some types of wish, however, are not so simple and the evaluation of their meaning is an impossible task. Such a wish might be for the love of one's parents. It cannot be said that such love is always assured, witness the numerous court cases of parents charged with the neglect of their children. Yet the wish for such love is recognized in

Freudian theories: it is one of the oldest, strongest and most insistent wishes of mankind. If such a wish existed but the child was uncertain of the love, there is no sure test, of the type demanded by Freud, to show whether or not love were present. There might be overt signs of affection, there might be gifts for the children, but the cynic at least could always suggest other motives than those of love for such behaviour. The parents might be trying to secure the support of their children during their old age, or it might be suggested that the affection which the parents appeared to show had its roots in the Oedipus complex. In fact there is scarcely any limit to the explanations which might be put forward. The child, on the other hand, not only wishes for love, but usually makes up his mind whether or not he is loved. On the whole his decision is probably correct. The basis on which he comes to this decision is that it alone makes sense of the relationship as he experiences it. There is no question of proof as in the case of Konstanz, but there is a belief or disbelief in the existence of the love according to the values the child finds in the relationship.

Freud would probably have replied to this that wishes are healthy and useful provided that the possibility of their fulfilment exists. Otherwise they are a waste of energy. He might have said that this illustration of the difficulty which the child finds in applying reality testing to the question of whether or not he is loved by the parent has no bearing on wish-fulfilment in religion. His only reason, however, for such an attitude would be his final decision that religion was an illusion in the ordinary sense of the word. He did not consider the problem of the kind of reality testing which would be necessary in order to prove or disprove religious doctrine. What his position really amounted to was this: religious doctrines are completely false, and wishing them to be true is wasting time instead of facing reality.

VIII

Freud faced the world as he saw it, and apparently never considered seriously the possibility that religious doctrines might contain some degree of truth. What he never fully allowed for was that the religious believer also faces the world as he sees it, only weighing the possibility that his religious interpretation might be wrong much more frequently than Freud allowed for. The believer has often been the first to say that he cannot prove the truth of the doctrines but that in the end he has to choose what appears to be the meaning of existence, and the conclusion he arrives at is a belief or faith. He might explain that Freud's disbelief in the truth of religious doctrine could be no more proved to be in correspondence with reality than his own religious faith. In religious belief there is frequently much more reality testing than Freud ever appreciated.

J. C. Flugel in his *Man, Morals and Society* (1945) has a chapter on "Wishful Thinking, Autism, and Unrealism" which, coming from one of the most prominent interpreters of psychoanalysis, is of very great interest. He writes:

Two further considerations should perhaps be borne in mind in assessing the value of 'wishful' as contrasted with 'realistic' thinking. The one relates to the general difficulty of knowing the 'real' and being able to distinguish it from the wishful, the phantastic, the illusory. Psychologists, and perhaps still more psychopathologists, are nearly always anxious to avoid philosophical questions, and when we read the literature on autism, the pleasure principle, the reality principle, etc., we may occasionally harbour justifiable suspicions that the metaphysical and epistemological aspects of the problems involved are being somewhat cavalierly treated—and this in spite of the fact that child analysts have considerably stressed the difficulty in learning to distinguish between the self and the not-self in the early days of life. But it remains true that in psychology it is possible to go a long way without coming too obviously and uncomfortably near these questions. In mental science, as in physical science and in ordinary life, we employ the various criteria of truth—'consistency' with our own and others' knowledge, 'correspondence' with supposed objective standards, and the 'pragmatic' test of 'does it work?'—with a somewhat liberal impartiality and a lighthearted reference to our own convenience. On the whole the method serves us fairly well, but the progress of science in recent times has shown the possibility of so many things that but a little earlier would have been thought impossible that it behoves us to adopt an attitude of caution and humility in dealing with the aspirations of those whom we might be inclined to dismiss as cranks, dreamers, or fanatics, utterly oblivious of the limitations imposed by the real world.[21]

Freud was drawing attention to a matter of great importance when he insisted that we should allow fully for the rôle of wish-fulfilment. But he was not asserting anything new—although he revealed some of the processes by which wish-fulfilment expresses itself. Demosthenes was clearly aware of the place of wish-fulfilment when he wrote: "What each man wishes, that also he thinks." Seneca knew that the reaction to frustration and an unfriendly environment is often the creation of fantasy: "What the wretched wish for intensely, that they believe without difficulty." And possibly the words "The wish is father to the thought" was a proverb before Shakespeare said "Thy wish was father, Harry, to that thought".* Dryden too was aware of the place of wish-fulfilment: "With how much ease believe we what we wish";† and Young expresses the same thought, "What ardently we wish, we soon believe".‡

Religious thinkers and prophets have constantly emphasized the danger of believing in false gods, of idolatry which is always a creation of our own desires. "For all the gods of the nations are idols: but the Lord made the heavens."§

---

* *King Henry the Fourth: Part II*, Act iv, Sc. 5.　　† *All for Love.*
‡ *The Complaint.*　　§ Ps. xcvi. 5.

The religious, like the irreligious, are subject to the temptations of wishful thinking. Meditation and self-examination have had their firm place in the practice of the religious life, and no limits have been set to their operation. The impulse to wishful thinking is no respecter of persons, and rigid adherence to psychoanalysis does not save one from its dangers. The acceptance of the arguments of psychoanalysis must be an act of faith, because there are no infallible proofs of their absolute truth. To say that the only reason for non-acceptance is that wishes lead to other systems of belief is no answer, for the same argument applies to the adherents of psychoanalysis.

The likelihood of wishful thinking should be recognized in every part of life and by all believers and thinkers. But its existence does not prove the validity or otherwise of belief in religion, psychoanalysis or anything else. Wishes point in as many directions as there are human beings. None is free from their influence, least of all he who thinks he is.

Instead of pointing to the dangers of wishful thinking in all realms of thought in *The Future of an Illusion*, Freud attempted to account for religious belief as the creation of man's wish to escape from stern reality. There was much which he did not examine and too much which he assumed. One assumption was his belief that he knew the nature of the limits of reality. Obsessed as he was with the problems of physical existence and the boundless progress which science made possible, such other realms as there might be were for him purely dependent ones, little if anything more than shadowy sublimations of energy drawn from sexual sources. Because his concept of reality was so narrow he attempted to explain too much in terms of wishful thinking; and his attempt was probably a functioning of his own wishful thinking—his wish to explain everything in terms of his child and idol, psychoanalysis.

IX

Freud maintained that one of the ways in which wish-fulfilments manifest themselves is through projection. Warren, in his

Dictionary of Psychology, defines the psychoanalytical use of this term as "the tendency or act of ascribing to the external world repressed mental processes which are not recognized as being of personal origin, as a result of which the content of these processes is experienced as an outer perception (e.g. the mechanism of delusions of persecution)". P. M. Symonds, in his *Dynamic Psychology*, gives a still simpler definition: "As most commonly used, projection is the reference of impulses, thoughts, feelings, and wishes originating in the person himself to persons and objects in the outside world."[22]

In Chapter 4 of *The Future of an Illusion* Freud gave his explanation of the way in which he believed that projection creates gods. When man personifies the forces of nature he follows an infantile prototype: "He has learnt from the persons of his earliest environment that the way to influence them is to establish a relationship with them, and so, later on, with the same end in view, he deals with everything that happens to him as he dealt with those persons."[23] Primitive man especially deals with the forces of nature in this way for he feels that he can deal with them just as he does with people. The forces of nature can be bribed, implored, flattered and threatened and gradually they come to be looked upon as gods. Man believes that he can understand the nature of what is external to himself, but what he really does is to interpret this according to the nature of his own psyche.

The term projection was used by Freud to describe an unconscious process used as a defence against external reality, or to preserve the ego. When he said that the beliefs in most religions arise by projections he implied that they are therefore likely to be false, because they are divorced from reality. They can be, and there often is an incorrect interpretation of what is external to us caused by a morbid and unhealthy condition in the unconscious, the motive of which is to escape reality and fashion it anew according to our own wishes. The distinction, however, between projection and some types of conscious thinking is probably not so clear-cut as Freud's assertions would suggest. For instance, we judge the behaviour of others according to what we know of our own, and we may be perfectly aware of what we are doing. We know that when we behave in a certain way we are jealous or angry, and when we see behaviour in others which is similar to our own we make the assumption that they too are jealous or angry.

What is external to ourselves has to be interpreted by a subject. Freud understood well enough the nature of pathological projection, but in this case he does not appear to have allowed for its normal operation. Moreover, he evidently thought of projection as functioning in an isolated way, and indeed with primitive man it probably did function largely in that manner. With man at a more advanced stage, however, there is constant reality testing of the results of the projection, and it is difficult to decide where the projections leave off and the testing begins. Projection is something like the application of a hypothesis in science for both are attempts to arrive at the truth. A scientist forms his hypothesis and applies it where it is relevant so that it can either be proved to be true or shown to be false unless, of course, judgment has to be suspended until conclusive evidence is available. In other words, there must be a sifting process. Projection has its place in science even as hypotheses have. An instance of this is the law of cause and effect, or the principle of causation. We have the experience of ourselves as causes, and we project this to the world outside ourselves and understand, so we believe, the nature of cause and effect.

Freud interpreted reality in materialistic terms, and even in this interpretation there were elements of projection. The religious believer has every right to question Freud's use of the word reality and he will contend that it is more than the materialistic universe postulated by Freud. He believes that his desires which act as pointers towards the nature of reality are as valid as those which urge the scientist to explore. He believes that he is testing and sifting and is prepared to respond in a completely cogent way to what he believes to be the nature of reality. Further, he would say that only by this sifting process can he discover whether his beliefs are justified or should be rejected,

G

and only in this way can he find meaning and purpose in life.

There is, of course, no guarantee that the religious believer is not sometimes mistaken about the nature of what he calls the supernatural world. Indeed the religious beliefs of a large number of people are influenced by false projections, and such people create narrow and inadequate gods out of the inadequacies of their own natures. It is this fact which frequently makes them so intolerant of the views held by those who differ from them. There are false gods created by crude, unconscious projections, as Freud rightly insisted. In fact all names, symbols and representations of God or gods must be cautiously used for, of their very nature, they must be limited and imperfect, and can easily attract to themselves inadequate projections. This is even true of the term Father when applied to God. It can be used by some believers in such a way that they apply the experience of their father too exclusively in their conception of God, so that He is too much of the 'exalted Father'. Where, however, it is clear that projection has played a large part in forming a concept of God or gods we should beware of making the judgment that everything is false about these projections, for mixed up with much that may be false there may still be elements of truth. A person who believes in a number of gods might be nearer the truth than one who says that there is no God at all. The enlightened religious believer, however, holds no brief for false gods. It can even readily be admitted that if what Freud described as religion covers all that religion is, it ought to be destroyed. Nothing can save the projected gods of primitive man or our own false gods.

The religious believer and thinker, no less than the believer and thinker in every other realm, has to be on the look-out for the elements of illusion bound up with the results of his own wishful thinking. Yet many of those who believe in religion and have written about it are familiar with the process of projection and are suspicious of wishful thinking in this realm. They know that it would tend to create a comfortable, cosy, and wholly inadequate idea of God.

The idea of God is the result to some extent of projection, for there is no other way in which such an idea could be formed. It is, however, an unwarranted assumption to say that because the idea is projected there is no corresponding God. If God is real, man could only come into contact with His reality in his own experience, and it does not follow that because our idea of God must arise in this way, it must be an illusion. This idea like all other ideas has, independently of its source, to be subjected to sifting and testing.

The intelligent believer knows that even if the existence of a supernatural world could be proved he is not likely to be infallible in his interpretations of it. Otherwise there would be no place for religious faith, which in itself he believes to be one of the supreme spiritual values. The presence of wishes leading to projections and even some illusions, of what are clearly no more than approximations to the truth, are not in themselves a denial that truth exists. Even limited and clearly imperfect religious beliefs may point to truer ones. A million wrong guesses do not prove that there is not a right one. All these possibilities are indeed only to be expected because the whole history of science proves clearly that the existence of the physical world is no guarantee that scientists will not make mistakes about it. Because they cannot know all about the world they do not stop trying to discover what they can. The history of science is a history of approximations, of hypotheses giving way to more probable ones, of so-called laws being replaced by others, for the human mind is not infallible in any realm.

The process of projection is a more complicated one than Freud admitted and is not so divorced from the other activities of the mind as he assumed. The religious believer who has attempted to make allowance for crude and inadequate projections may believe that the act of projection through which man attempts to know God may have its source not in himself but in God. The so-called projecting may not be man making God, but rather the disclosure of God Himself. He would claim that it is a way in which God is primarily seeking man rather than man, through wish-fulfilment, creating the image of God.

X

Freud was well aware that the mind is often sifting and testing to allow for the possibility of projections and the beliefs associated with them, but he was deeply suspicious of much of its reasoning which he thought is largely determined by wishes. As far as religion is concerned he would have said that man first wishes for God and then invents reasons for belief in His existence. The same process, which psychoanalysts call rationalization, is thus responsible for religious dogma. Freud reacted to the rationalism of his own age and, indeed, of the ages which preceded it, and he saw clearly that reason was not the cold, unmoved principle which it is often held to be. On the whole, he maintained, men and women do not reason objectively, but reasoning powers are largely used in the service of unconscious motives.

A lucid exposition of the psychoanalytical view of rationalization is given by Ernest Jones in Chapter 2, "Rationalization in Everyday Life", of his *Psychoanalysis*. Dr. Jones pointed out that the large majority of conscious mental processes in a normal person arise from sources unsuspected by him and that feeling underlies them. At the same time there are concealment mechanisms, so that the thinker is not aware that his so-called reasons are the product of wishes and desires which lie deep in the unconscious. The form taken by religious beliefs, Jones declared, is one of the clearest examples of the form of evasion known as rationalization. A number of arguments is used by each sect to support its own interpretation of religion, and although the reasons given may be unconvincing to outsiders they appear completely convincing to a member of that sect. Jones gives as an example a man brought up with a very strong Baptist background. When he reaches puberty he may become a Baptist and scarcely give a second thought to the question, but after a time it may occur to him that this is irrational, and that he ought not to hold a belief merely because his family and acquaintances do. With every sign of reason and objectivity he determines to undertake a critical and dispassionate examination of the evidence for and against being a Baptist. Actually, in spite of all his protestations of objectivity, he is only seeking pretexts to remain in the fold. When he has found sufficient reasons he asserts that he has become convinced of the truth of the Baptists' position by all the evidence which he has so carefully studied, and if he were accused of being a Baptist because of his background he would deny this completely unacceptable explanation. The real origin of his beliefs, according to Dr. Jones, was concealed from him by the process of rationalization. We should realize this if we presented the arguments which had been so convincing to the Baptist to a Roman Catholic, by whom they would be rejected as being obviously false and unconvincing. Jones comes to the conclusion: "We are beginning to see man not as the smooth, self-acting agent he pretends to be, but as he really is—a creature only dimly conscious of the various influences that mould his thought and action, and blindly resisting with all the means at his command the forces that are making for a higher and fuller consciousness."[24] Rationalization is essentially a defence mechanism which enables us to maintain our self-regard and our pride and our system of beliefs in spite of all opposition.

Even when our brains work with apparently perfect logic there can still be rationalization. We give undue prominence to a fact in one place and close our eyes to other facts and then, in the end, produce a result which accords entirely with our unconscious desires. This applies to religious belief as to other realms such as politics, economics and psychology. Nor is science exempt, as Bacon realized when he said: "Man makes a science to his liking". Freud's argument that man rationalizes more about religious belief than about other subjects is a very doubtful assumption, to say the least. The really important point, however, is the extent to which religious doctrines are the result of rationalization. As we have said, extreme forms of sectarianism owe much of their structure to rationalization, and religious believers in general do recognize this fact. A typical member of a religious community does not think that he has a monopoly of the truth, but for reasons of his upbringing, temperament and so on, the particular denomination to which he belongs will probably remain his, although it is quite common to move from one communion to another. But in a predominantly Christian country the form of religion followed continues to be Christian. In a Moslem country the form of religion which is practised will be Islam, and so on.

Before religious belief is condemned as mere rationalization it is well to keep in mind that perhaps the place of rationalization in religious matters has not been so underrated as Freud thought. Jeremiah was surely referring to the same process when he said: "The heart is deceitful above all things, and desperately wicked: who can know it?" (XVII. 9). Self-examination and meditation have had prominent places in most religions, other than very primitive ones. Some forms of preaching clearly help to strengthen rationalizations, but other forms endeavour to clear them away so that the truth shall make men free.

Further, the well-informed religious believer sees beyond the boundaries of his own communion. Within Christianity, for instance, oecumenical movements have been increasing. Even wider than that, the Christian believer often sees much truth and much to admire in other religious faiths, for example those of Islam and of the East. The religious believer does not believe nearly as much as is sometimes suspected that he has a monopoly of the truth.

Nor must the rational elements underlying much of religious faith be under-estimated. When rationalization has been allowed for, rational arguments and the facts of history have to be considered. As far as the Christian Faith is concerned there are arguments for the existence of God and for the truth of the creeds. The Christian believer can attempt to discover the facts about the life of Jesus Christ and about His death and reported resurrection. There are cases where arguments and the historical facts have converted people into believing, despite preconceived theories and unconscious wishes. Rationalization may have supported another structure but this has been driven out by the weight of evidence in favour of the Christian Faith.

The concept of rationalization must not be pushed too far for it cannot explain all religious beliefs, philosophies and psychologies. If all reasoning is basically rationalization then it must be argued that psychoanalysis itself is the result of this process, and that it has no other significance. In fact it would be impossible to approach truth in any direction if conscious thinking consisted of nothing more than rationalization.

Rationalization itself has often been misunderstood, and in using this term we must be on our guard against treating man as largely irrational. It is true that the outside observer sometimes finds what appears to him to be irrational beliefs in others. Physicists may find this in the beliefs held by some people about the shape of the world, or economists may discover beliefs which do not accord with the facts as they know them. From the psychological point of view, however, people are often not so irrational as they seem. Their beliefs can change as a result of rational arguments and the search for facts may lead to more convincing beliefs. Such possibilities appear to be a part of the mental life of almost everyone. Man often rationalizes because he wants his world to appear reasonable. We find, for example, in some psychological experiments on perception that a man distorts and selects facts in order to produce a reasonable result. Therefore rationalization is not a sign of man's irrationality but, on the contrary, evidence for his innate rationality. Man all the time strives to find reasons because he is striving for intellectual consistency in his own psychological world. Freud does not appear to have recognized the extent to which beliefs are due to man's continual search for meaning. We are all the time striving to discover meaning, perhaps unconsciously as well as consciously. Where beliefs in a particular area of life are only vaguely formulated or structured, man will continue to search for meaning, and frequently he will change his beliefs so that they have more meaning. It is actually part of education to encourage such a search. Man also deals with his needs in the same way, for he wants to understand them and the reasons which he finds even in this part of his life are frequently not mere rationalizations, but structures which give significance to his needs.

Freud, in asserting his belief in the possibilities of science, implied that reason, which is at the base of scientific procedure, has a very real place. He was concerned with making allowance for the motives in the unconscious which hinder the clear working of reason. Such, then, are the unconscious desires and wishes which give rise to the processes of projection and rationalization. Freud believed that in forming his religious beliefs man is largely under the influence of these motives and processes. This point is particularly important for no criticism which Freud made of religion is more searching. Man is apt to be led astray by his wishes and to create systems in accord with them. The truth of this matter has never been more forcibly expressed than in the words of the Sermon on the Mount, "Blessed are the pure in heart for they shall see God."

Although Freud was undoubtedly sincere he dealt inadequately with religion in *The Future of an Illusion*. He attempted to explain too much in terms of wish-fulfilment, projection and rationalization. Whatever place these processes may occupy, the question of the truth or falsity of religion is an altogether different issue. Moreover, Freud looked at the experiences of religion in an extroverted and limited way and omitted purposely all consideration of emotions as though they were always nefarious.

NOTES TO CHAPTER 4

[1] S. Freud, *The Future of an Illusion*, trans. W. D. Robson-Scott. London, Hogarth Press (1949), p. 12.
[2] *Ibid.*, pp. 12-13.
[3] *Ibid.*, p. 25.
[4] *Ibid.*, pp. 36-7.
[5] *Ibid.*, p. 43.
[6] *Ibid.*, p. 48.

[7] *Ibid.*, p. 45.

[8] *Ibid.*, p. 51.

[9] *Ibid.*, p. 52.

[10] *Ibid.*, p. 53.

[11] *Ibid.*, p. 55.

[12] *Ibid.*, p. 55.

[13] *Ibid.*, pp. 56-7.

[14] *Ibid.*, p. 57.

[15] *Ibid.*, p. 58.

[16] *Ibid.*, pp. 67-8.

[17] T. Reik, *From Thirty Years with Freud*. London, Hogarth Press (1942), p. 123.

[18] S. Freud, *op. cit.*, p. 86.

[19] *Ibid.*, p. 95.

[20] *Ibid.*, p. 98.

[21] J. C. Flugel, *Man, Morals and Society*. London, Duckworth (1945), pp. 232-3.

[22] P. M. Symonds, *Dynamic Psychology*. New York, Appleton-Century-Crofts (1949), p. 223.

[23] S. Freud, *op. cit.*, p. 38.

[24] Ernest Jones, *Papers on Psycho-Analysis*, 3rd. edn. London, Baillière Tindall & Cox (1923), p. 15.

5

Moses and Monotheism

"But we venture to be independent of the historians in other respects and to blaze our own trail."

SIGMUND FREUD, *Moses and Monotheism* (p. 60).

I

FREUD'S last book was concerned with the subject in which, during the latter part of his life, he had shown so great an interest—religion. For many years he had planned a vast work which would apply psychoanalytical theories to the whole of the Bible. *Moses and Monotheism* was the only part of it which he was able to complete. He had always been particularly interested in Moses, and when he visited Rome he was fascinated by Michelangelo's famous statue and wrote a paper on this subject in 1914 which, curiously enough, he published anonymously.

The theme of *Moses and Monotheism* is an astonishing one, even for a Jew who did not accept the faith of his fathers. Briefly it is as follows: Moses was not a Jew but an Egyptian, and Jewish monotheism was derived from Egypt, in particular from a period of pure monotheism established during the reign of Ikhnaton. Freud believed that Moses was the son, presumably illegitimate, of one of the daughters of a Pharaoh, and that he lived in Egypt during the period immediately following Ikhnaton. Because of his birth he was a person of great importance; possibly he had been governor of a province and as such had come into touch with the Israelites. In his zeal as a reformer Ikhnaton had attempted to stamp out the popular religion, and after his death there was a tremendous revolt against all that he had stood for. Moses was an adherent of Ikhnaton, but because of the revolution he was not able to practise, at least openly, the form of religion in which he believed. He therefore decided to free the Israelites from Egypt and to train them in the monotheistic religion of Ikhnaton. This he did, but after a period (it is not known how long) the Israelites revolted and killed him. After at least two generations, and probably somewhat longer, the Israelites had another leader to whom also they gave the name of Moses and it was he, the second Moses, who gave them their Yahweh religion. But the teaching of the first Moses, the Egyptian, remained a latent force in the racial unconscious of the Israelites and was responsible for the monotheism of the prophets and people hundreds of years later. In fact it was only then that the teaching of the first Moses emerged in all its purity.

In the killing of the first Moses we have another example of the slaying of the primal father, and a sense of guilt about it remained in the racial unconscious. The significance of the death of Jesus was that it was an atonement by one of the brothers for the slaying of the father. Salvation was obtained through the sacrifice of Jesus, and Christianity became a religion based on the son rather than on the stern father. The Holy Communion has the importance of the primitive totem feast and is in a direct line of descent from it.

II

Biblical and other scholars who have studied this period are well aware of the problems connected with Moses, the Exodus and its date, the different views about the period of Ikhnaton's reign and the development of Hebrew monotheism. These are realms in which there is ample room for speculation and Freud speculated to the full. Indeed he himself wrote, in discussing the supposed murder of the first Moses and the date of a second Moses, "as we know that in our hypothesis one assumption only rests on another we have to admit that this discussion shows a weak spot in the construction".[1] Anyone who has studied the processes of perception knows that where the field of perception is ambiguous there is the greatest variation in what is seen. The deciding factor is usually what is expected or desired, a fact recognized and taken advantage of by every conjuror. By the unconscious selection of the most unlikely hypotheses, and the ignoring of all material which was contrary to his main contentions, Freud produced a thesis which appeared to him to be convincing as an exposition of the theories of psychoanalysis applied to this particular realm.

The general consensus of opinion among scholars in this field is well expressed by one of the most eminent of them, W. F. Albright, in his *From the Stone Age to Christianity* ("Monotheism and the Historical Process"): "As a counterpoise to these serious, though exaggerated, theories we may be pardoned for saying a word about a futile but widely read example of psychological determinism—Freud's *Moses and Monotheism* (1939). This book is simply the latest of a long train of books and papers on history and religion which have been issued by Freud himself and other members of the psychoanalytical school during the past generation. Like them his new book is totally devoid of serious historical method and deals with historical data even more cavalierly than with the data of introspective and experimental psychology."[2]

Allowance must be made, of course, for the conditions under which this book was written. Parts I and II were published in German in 1937 when Freud was over eighty, and nearly the whole of Part III was rewritten in London from June, 1938, and although this was more than half the whole book it was completed within about six weeks after his arrival—according to a report published by H. W. Puner.[3] During the planning of the book in Vienna he was surrounded by bitter anti-Semitism. His books were burnt and his publishing house destroyed; his whole future and that of his children were in danger. There was every kind of disturbance and a real fear of persecution, and in the middle of the writing of this book came the move to England. As if this were not enough there was the long-standing and painful cancer of the mouth and, of course, there was old age.

All these things must have had their effect and are at least partly responsible for the fact that this is the most ill-arranged, discursive, repetitive and unconvincing of all his works.

III

Freud himself was convinced that Moses was an Egyptian, but curiously enough he calls Part I "Moses, an Egyptian", and Part II "If Moses was an Egyptian". He gives four lines of argument for the contention that Moses was an Egyptian:

1. The name Moses was Egyptian.
2. The story of his birth takes the form of a typical myth which, rightly interpreted, would on psychological grounds suggest that he was an Egyptian.
3. He introduced circumcision, a specifically Egyptian rite, to the Israelites.
4. He was "slow of speech" because he spoke Egyptian and therefore needed an interpreter.

IV

Now let us see what evidence he brought forward to support his contention. He discussed the name Moses at some length and relied on the work of J. H. Breasted, author of the well-known *History of Egypt* and other works. He quoted from *The Dawn of Conscience* where Breasted considered the name Moses and came to the clear conclusion that

... it is simply an Egyptian word "mose" meaning "child", and is an abridgement of a fuller form of such names as "Amen mose" meaning "Amon-a-child" or "Ptah-mose", meaning "Ptah-a-child", these forms themselves being likewise abbreviations for the complete form "Amon-(has-given)-a child" or "Ptah-(has-given)-a-child". The abbreviation "child" early became a convenient rapid form for the cumbrous full name, and the name Mose, "child", is not uncommon on Egyptian monuments. The father of Moses without doubt prefixed to his son's name that of an Egyptian god like Amon or Ptah, and this divine name was gradually lost in current usage, till the boy was called "Mose". (The final *s* is an addition drawn from the Greek translation of the Old Testament. It is not in the Hebrew, which has "mosheh").[4]

The narrative in Exodus represents the name Moses as coming from the Hebrew *mashah* 'to draw', but it is now generally agreed that the word was Egyptian in derivation and so Freud was right in following Breasted and concluding that Moses had an Egyptian name. This, however, does not make him necessarily a member of that nation, for many of the Israelites bore Egyptian names such as Assir, Pashur, Hophni, Phinehas, and Merari.

Although, therefore, the name of Moses is certainly Egyptian, there are explanations for this which fit in well with the Old Testament narratives. If a daughter of Pharaoh adopted a Jewish boy, who, because of the circumstances of his adoption, was nameless, she would naturally give him an Egyptian name. Every tradition points to a lengthy sojourn of the Israelites in Egypt and, as we have seen, this left its impression in a legacy of Egyptian names which in themselves meant little. Unless this was an accepted fact the name Moses would hardly have been retained for the Israelitish national hero. If, as Freud contended, we are dealing with a myth by which the Hebrews attempted to conceal the Egyptian origin of Moses, they would surely have suppressed his Egyptian name if it had had all the significance he attributed to it. Moses was so decidedly an Israelite that his Egyptian name could be retained, and in fact becomes an argument in favour of the substantial historicity of the traditional story of Moses and of his Israelite origin. From the Israelite standpoint there was nothing to hide.

V

Anyone studying the Moses story must consider the possibility of myth playing some part, and Freud believed that it played a large part. In fact he concluded that it gave a psychological reason for the contention that Moses was an Egyptian. He maintained that there is an 'average myth' for which a formula can be constructed. The hero is the child of high-ranking parents, usually the son of a king. Before his birth his father is warned by an oracle or dream that the child will be a danger to himself. The father arranges for the babe to be killed or exposed, and usually the myth takes the form that the babe is placed in a casket and exposed to the waves. The child is then saved by animals or poor people such as shepherds, and suckled by a female animal or a woman of humble birth. After many adventures he finds his noble parents when he is full grown, takes vengeance on his father, and, coming into his birthright, achieves fame. Freud gave Sargon, Moses, Cyrus and Romulus as conforming in part at least to this average myth.

Superficially the story of Moses appears to be very different from the average myth. The first family, usually so distinguished, is a modest one for he is the child of Jewish Levites, whereas the second family, usually the humble one, is replaced by the royal house of Egypt. Freud met this difficulty by referring to E. Meyer and others who supposed that the original form of the myth was different. In this Pharaoh has been warned in a prophetic dream that his daughter's son would become a danger to him and his kingdom, and it was Pharaoh who delivered Moses to the waters of the Nile soon after his birth. The child was then saved by a Jewish family and brought up as their own.

Freud recognized that this reconstruction of the myth is not convincing, for the myth would have to be either of Egyptian or Jewish origin. We can exclude its Egyptian origin because there would be no motive here to make Moses into a hero. The Jews would not produce such a legend for it would make their hero into an alien. The only part of the myth which appears to apply is the feature which makes the child survive in spite of strong forces desiring its destruction.

Freud then considered the two families in the myth and concluded:

> As we know, on the level of analytic interpretation they are identical. On a mythical level they are distinguished as the noble and the humble family. With an historical person to whom the myth has become attached there is, however, a third level, that of reality. One of the families is the real one, the one into which the great man was really born and in which he was brought up. The other is fictitious, invented by the myth in pursuance of its own motives. As a rule the real family corresponds with the humble one, the noble family with the fictitious one. In the case of Moses something seemed to be different. And here the new point of view may perhaps bring some illumination. It is that the first family, the one from which the babe is exposed to danger, is in all comparable cases the fictitious one; the second family, however, by which the hero is adopted and in which he grows up, is his real one. If we have the courage to accept this statement as a general truth to which the Moses legend also is subject, then we suddenly see our way clear. Moses is an Egyptian—probably of noble origin— whom the myth undertakes to transform into a Jew. And that would be our conclusion! The exposure in the water was in its right place; to fit the new conclusion the intention had to be changed, not without violence. From a means of getting rid of the child it becomes a means of its salvation.[5]

He justified this interpretation by considering the special feature in the life of Moses which makes the legend different: "Moses began by descending from his eminence to the level of the children of Israel".[6] But he seems to have held a very much exaggerated view of the eminence of Moses both at the time of his birth and later. He represented him as an "august Egyptian" and stated: "It is not credible that a great gentleman

like the Egyptian Moses approached a people strange to him
without an escort. He must have brought his retinue with him,
his nearest adherents, his scribes, his servants. These were the
original Levites."[7] Such a statement involves many assumptions.
First that he was an Egyptian, secondly an extremely august one,
thirdly that he brought a retinue with him and fourthly that these
were the original Levites. Freud's postulate also assumed that
the Biblical narratives are not to be relied upon for there we have
a picture of a Moses who was perfectly free to move about
and see for himself exactly what was happening. In this way
he saw the cruel treatment accorded to his fellow-countrymen
and he even killed one of the oppressing Egyptians, but there
was no retinue to see him, only his own countrymen. He escaped
to Midian and lived there, married and had a son. It was only after
the death of the Egyptian king who was on the throne at the time
of his escape that he returned and made the attempt to free his
people. This is no picture of an august Egyptian accompanied
by his impressive retinue. Moses was a man humble enough
to help the seven daughters of the priest of Midian to water
their flocks.

It is, indeed, doubtful if Moses ever was the august personage
imagined by Freud. It has commonly been supposed that the
rescuer of Moses was a daughter of Rameses II who is said to have
had no fewer than fifty-nine daughters. Even if we cannot be
sure that fifty-nine is the correct number, or even that Rameses II
was the Pharaoh of the oppression, this tradition suggests that
a Pharaoh of that period, being a polygynist, often had an
extremely large family. Therefore it is improbable that an adopted
son or an illegitimate one, or even a legitimate son of one of the
numerous daughters, would be an august person except as the
result of his own efforts. In the Biblical records Moses is represented as a Jew and it is true that succeeding generations of
Jews would like to think of the acknowledged founder of their
race as being a member of it. This very natural wish does not
affect the facts, and in itself is no sound foundation on which
to build a theory that he was a member of another race.

Moses was not a hero by virtue of his august birth but because of his achievements in delivering his people from the bondage of Egypt, and becoming their leader and lawgiver. There are great differences, too, between the Moses story and the other myths to which Freud compared it. The others were clearly myths, whereas the story of Moses approaches more closely recorded facts. It is true that the Moses story was not written in its present form until anything from 300 to 500 years later, but the oral tradition by which it was transmitted did not cover a sufficiently long period to account for the degree of distortion imagined by Freud. A live oral tradition of this nature which persists for so long is usually more reliable than Freud would have us suppose. W. F. Albright in *From the Stone Age to Christianity* has a section on the characteristics of oral tradition (pp. 33-43), and his concluding sentence is: "We can hardly, therefore, be surprised to find archaeological discoveries confirming Israelite tradition almost always, *as far as they go*."[8] Interpretations of the Moses material as myth are too uncertain to be used as a basis for any theory, and certainly for such a one as that Moses was an Egyptian.

VI

Circumcision had long been practised in Egypt and Freud believed that Moses brought it from there, using this point as further evidence for his Egyptian theory: "If Moses gave the Jews not only a new religion, but also the law of circumcision, he was no Jew but an Egyptian, and then the Mosaic religion was probably an Egyptian one, namely—because of its contrast to the popular religion—that of Aton with which the Jewish one shows agreement in some remarkable points."[9] He also states, "The fact remains that the question concerning the origin of circumcision has only one answer: it comes from Egypt. Herodotus, 'the Father of History', tells us that the custom of circumcision had long been practised in Egypt, and his statement has been confirmed by the examination of mummies and even by drawings on the walls of graves. No other people of the

Eastern Mediterranean has—as far as we know—followed this custom; we can assume with certainty that the Semites, Babylonians and Sumerians were not circumcised."[10]

If Freud had fully examined his own authority, the Father of History, he would have found that there is a passage in Herodotus which states that the rite was practised by Phoenicians, Hittites, Ethiopians, as well as by the Egyptians. More significant still, there is evidence that circumcision was practised among the early Semites long before the Mosaic age. There is evidence in the Hebrew names for father-in-law and son-in-law to show that among the early Semites it was an initiatory rite to marriage. The use of a flint instrument also points to its antiquity. Again there is the story that on his way back to Egypt Moses was smitten because he had not been circumcised before marriage, but his Kenite wife, Zipporah, saved him by circumcising their child and so circumcising Moses by proxy. This would suggest that circumcision was a Kenite practice and that Moses derived it from there. The part which Zipporah played is surely significant, and it was made so important an issue in his own family circle before Moses returned to Egypt that we can understand the place he gave to it when laying down the law and future practice of his people. If Moses brought the rite of circumcision from Egypt it appears strange that he himself is represented as not being circumcised. The source of circumcision in general and the origins of the Hebrew practice of circumcision are far more complex than Freud assumed.

VII

Freud also maintained that Moses was called 'slow of speech' because he was a foreigner and so needed an interpreter:

Another trait imputed to him deserves our special interest. Moses was said to have been 'slow of speech'—that is to say, he must have had a speech impediment or inhibition—so that he had to call on Aaron (who is called his brother) for assistance in his supposed discussions with Pharaoh. This again may be historical truth and would serve as a welcome addition to the endeavour to make the picture of this great man live. It may, however, have another and more important significance. The report may, in a slightly distorted way, recall the fact that Moses spoke another language and was not able to communicate with his Semitic Neo-Egyptians without the help of an interpreter—at least not at the beginning of their intercourse. Thus a fresh confirmation of the thesis: Moses was an Egyptian.[11]

But if Moses were Egyptian and spoke the language he would not need, as Freud admits, an interpreter to speak to Pharaoh. And it is for speaking to Pharaoh that the Biblical narratives represent Moses as needing a prophet to assist him: "And the Lord spake unto Moses saying, Go in, speak unto Pharaoh king of Egypt, that he let the children of Israel go out of his land. And Moses spake before the Lord, saying, Behold, the children of Israel have not hearkened unto me; how then shall Pharaoh hear me, who am of uncircumcised lips? And the Lord spake unto Moses and unto Aaron, and gave them a charge unto the children of Israel, and unto Pharaoh king of Egypt, to bring the children of Israel out of the land of Egypt."[12] "And the Lord said unto Moses, See, I have made thee a god to Pharaoh: and Aaron thy brother shall be thy prophet. Thou shalt speak all that I command thee: and Aaron thy brother shall speak unto Pharaoh, that he send the children of Israel out of his land."[13] The reasons for the slowness of speech are his diffidence and the fact that he is uncircumcised and so feels separated from the Egyptians and especially from Pharaoh. And, if the narrative can be relied upon at all, his inspired speaker or prophet is his own brother Aaron. It is on the flimsiest evidence that in all this Freud can find "a fresh confirmation of the thesis 'Moses was an Egyptian' ".

VIII

Freud represented Amenhotep IV, who came to the throne *circa* 1375 B.C., as a strong, impressive and indeed unique figure, who formulated a strict form of monotheism which, so far as we know, was the first attempt of its kind in history, quoting approvingly Breasted's well-known reference to him as "the first individual in history".

But as Freud well knew everything which appears to be new must have its roots in the past, including the reforms of Amenhotep IV. There was a school of priests in the sun temple at On (Heliopolis) in which there had long been tendencies leading to the idea of a universal god and stressing his ethical attributes. Under Amenhotep III, the father of the reformer, the worship of the sun god was in the ascendant and he was given his ancient name of Aton. It was in this Aton religion that Freud believed Amenhotep IV found his inspiration. Political conditions in Egypt also had their influence on religion. The great conquests of Thothmes III (1501-1447) which had made Egypt into a world power were reflected in religion as universalism and monotheism.

Amenhotep IV changed his name until it embodied that of the one God in whom he believed and so he was called Ikhnaton. A further stage in his reforms was to leave the old capital of Thebes and build a new one called Akhetaton (Horizon of Aton). He closed the old temples, forbade the holding of services, and proceeded to seize the property which belonged to the adherents of the old religion. His vigorous reforms created enemies and he encountered strong opposition, especially among the priests of Amon who had been powerful. Ikhnaton reigned for seventeen years but after his death he was regarded as a heretic and, in a violent reaction, this new religion was swept away and, as far as possible, every trace of it removed. He had no son and his successor, who was his son-in-law, the well-known Tutankhaton, was forced to return to Thebes and even to substitute Amon in his name for that of the god Aton. What Freud twice called "the glorious eighteenth dynasty" was at an end.

The amateur Egyptologist who studies the Ikhnaton period is almost certain to be both puzzled and fascinated, and perhaps much the same is true even of experts on this subject. However, the old view accepted by Freud that Ikhnaton was among the most remarkable men who ever lived, a man of genius who reformed the art and religion of Egypt, is no longer uncritically accepted. There are other completely contrary views which maintain that he was an effeminate, impractical dreamer, largely responsible for the disintegration of the empire, or else that he was the tool of others, for example his wife Nefretiti, his mother Tiji or a group of priests or reformers. A weakling in body, he was also, it is said, one in mind and spirit, and it is suggested that his so-called religious reforms had a political origin. They were the beginning of the development of a split with the powerful priesthood of Amon.

What is reasonably certain is that many of the earlier Egyptologists had a sentimental and romantic view of Ikhnaton and overstated the purity of the reforms which are associated with that period. This has been corrected by later scholars who have had the revealing excavations at Tell el-Amarna to assist them. Pendlebury, in *Tell el-Amarna*, says of Ikhnaton's religion: "To-day the impression that the art and civilization of Amarna gives us is that of an ephemeral butterfly age with that total lack of moral standards usually associated with happy morons. So much has been written about Akhenaten [Ikhnaton] in the character of a Christ before his time that it must be pointed out that Atonism was in no sense a way of life but merely an exercise in theology."[14]

Some scholars think that the father was more responsible for the development of Atonism than his son Ikhnaton, and it is probable that he was co-regent with his son for about nine years, and even that the city of Akhetaton was founded before Amenhotep III died and that he lived there for a period.

It is also probable that Nefretiti, his famous and beautiful queen, who provided another reason for sentimentalizing over Ikhnaton, was a devoted follower of Aton, though probably

Pendlebury was going too far when he said of Ikhnaton and Nefretiti, "to-day we should call them religious maniacs".[15] Possibly Nefretiti was the stronger devotee of the two, for if so this would explain some happenings in the obscure last years of Ikhnaton's reign when there was a terrible family quarrel ending in the disgrace of Nefretiti. She retired to the north end of the city, where she built herself a palace called Hat-Aten (the castle of the Aton). It is clear then that she did not desert Aton. But there are some grounds for thinking that Ikhnaton may have tried to compromise with the priests of Amon, for his half-brother, Smenkhkare, married his eldest daughter Meritaten and went to Thebes, reigning there as co-regent. In the third year of his reign he restored some form of Amon worship at Thebes. It has been sometimes suggested that the quarrel was over this: Ikhnaton was prepared to compromise but Nefretiti was not, hence the separation and the defiant name of her palace.

The Tell el-Amarna tablets show the empire falling to pieces. For instance the Habiru, probably Hebrew tribes, were gaining ground in Palestine and Abdi-Heba, the faithful governor of Jerusalem, repeatedly appealed to Ikhnaton for help but this was not sent. It has sometimes been said that probably the ministers concerned did not allow Ikhnaton to see this correspondence, but a ruler should be sufficiently in touch with events in his territories to know what was happening. The spreading disaster surely could not be hidden.

No wiser words could be spoken about this period than those of the modern Egyptian scholar J. A. Wilson in *Before Philosophy*: "Was the lofty revolution of Akhnaton against the all-embracing control of the old imperial gods—a revolution which used the slogan of *ma^cat*, 'justice'—a moral protest against the abuse of power or simply a political move to secure power for a new party? We cannot give final answers to these questions; the situation will never permit a simple arbitrary analysis; and our answers may arise out of personal prejudices."[16]

IX

It would seem that Freud not only exaggerated the place of Ikhnaton as a religious reformer, but that he probably simplified the Egyptian religion of the period, especially when he called it 'pure monotheism'.

The sun always had a dominating place in Egyptian thought and life because of its practical, powerful, day-to-day influence. It might be thought that with so much sun the darkness would be welcomed as giving protection. In fact the Egyptians hated darkness and they found their happiness in greeting the rising of the sun which was viewed as a source of light and life, and gradually the personification of the sun's power led to the belief in the sun-god who became the supreme creator god. There were other gods, but the sun, as the supreme god, lent himself to other gods to give "them a primacy within geographical or functional limits".[17]

Wilson believes that "the fluidity of Egyptian concepts and the tendency to synthesize divergent elements"[18] has been responsible for the contention that the Egyptians were monotheistic, that all the gods were subsumed into a single god. But he believes too that such views are wrong in that they simplify the actual position far too much, for "it is not a matter of single god but of single nature of observed phenomena in the universe, with the clear possibility of exchange and substitution. With relation to gods and men the Egyptians were monophysites: many men and many gods, but all ultimately of one nature."[19]

Although the Egyptians recognized different beings they felt that they were of a single essential substance, "a rainbow, in which certain colours were dominant under certain conditions and others dominant when the conditions altered. A complete personality includes many different aspects of personality."[20]

Meek in *Hebrew Origins* gives his verdict both about Ikhnaton and his possible influence on monotheism: "Instead of helping the cause of monotheism Akhenaten killed it by bringing the Egyptian movement toward monotheism to a head too soon, by making too great a break with the old religion, by resorting to force to establish his religion, and by dying too soon, leaving no efficient successor to carry on his work. If Akhenaten was not able to convert his own people in his lifetime, it is surely unthinkable that he was able after his death to impress an alien like Moses, particularly when Moses lived, as Albright agrees, in the period of bitter reaction against Akhenaten."[21]

X

Freud's chief reason for asserting that Moses was an Egyptian was his belief that Jewish monotheism was derived from "the monotheistic episode in Egyptian history" which is "the kernel of our thesis",[22] and Moses, Freud argued, was the link between the two. Indeed as he imaginatively reconstructed the background, his hypothesis was that Moses, a man of high rank and forceful in character, was an intimate follower of Ikhnaton, who turned to the Israelites, and attempted to preserve the Aton religion through them and to make them express all his religious ideals.

There is one difficulty in this hypothesis which Freud had to recognize and it would have daunted anyone less determined than he: the religion of the Mosaic age did not resemble the religion of the Ikhnaton period as presented by Freud or indeed by anyone else. As Freud himself put it: "These modern historians, well represented by E. Meyer, follow the Biblical text in one decisive point. They concur that the Jewish tribes, who later on became the people of Israel, at a certain time accepted a new religion. But this event did not take place in Egypt nor at the foot of a mount in the Sinai peninsula, but in a place called Meribat-Qadeš, an oasis distinguished by its abundance of springs and wells in the country south of Palestine between the eastern end of the Sinai peninsula and the western end of Arabia. There they took over the worship of a god Jahve, probably from the Arabic tribe of Midianites who lived near by. Presumably other neighbouring tribes were also followers of that god."[23]

This Jahve, Freud said, "was certainly a volcano god". The particular mountain may have been Sinai-Horeb which was believed to be Jahve's abode, and Freud, following Meyer, concluded that the original character of this god was that of "an uncanny, bloodthirsty demon who walks by night and shuns the light of day".[24] Most critics nowadays, as we shall see, do not give to Yahweh the character ascribed to him by Freud and the authorities whom he follows, but there is a common agreement that the religion of Yahweh cannot be associated with the Aton religion. Freud continued: "The mediator between the people and the god at this birth of a new religion was called Moses. He was the son-in-law of the Midianite priest Jethro and was tending his flocks when he received the divine summons. Jethro visited him in Qadeš to give him instructions."[25] It is small wonder that he added: "Our Egyptian Moses differs perhaps no less from the Midian Moses than the universal god Aton differed from the demon Jahve on his divine mountain. And if we concede any measure of truth to the information furnished by modern historians, then we have to admit that the thread we wished to draw from the surmise that Moses was an Egyptian has broken off for the second time; this time, so it seems, without any hope of its being tied again."[26]

He nevertheless believed that in spite of what the Biblical records had said, and all the information produced by modern historians, he had succeeded in tying the required knot. To do it, however, he had to produce two novel hypotheses: the first was that there was an Egyptian Moses who taught the Israelites the religion of Aton and a second Moses who lived sixty to a hundred years later who was the Midianite Moses and who gave the Israelites the Yahweh religion. There is not the slightest evidence for a second Moses and no one but Freud has ever suggested that there were two. He, however, thought that the suggestion made by Sellin in 1922 that Moses met a violent end in a rebellion of his stubborn and refractory people provided a way out of this difficulty. But Sellin thought that such a deed would have been carried out in Shittim in the land east of the

Jordan and this will not do, for "we shall see, however, that the choice of this locality does not accord with our argument".[27] So Freud adopted the suggestion that a Moses was killed by the Jews and that he was the Egyptian Moses. As for the rest "we venture to be independent of the historians in other respects and to blaze our own trail".[28] This he undoubtedly did. As the book proceeded the trail became a firmly established main road and the suggestion of Sellin became an unshakable fact, so that on p. 98 we read: "Out of the darkness which the Biblical Text has here left—or rather created—the historical research of our days can distinguish two facts. The first, discovered by E. Sellin, is that the Jews, who even according to the Bible were stubborn and unruly towards their lawgiver and leader, rebelled at last, killed him and threw off the imposed Aton religion as the Egyptians had done before them."[29] Yet on p. 59 Freud had said: "Naturally I am not in a position to decide whether Sellin has correctly interpreted the relevant passages in the prophets. If he is right, however, we may regard as historically credible the tradition he recognized: for such things are not readily invented—there is no tangible motive for doing so."[30] And the tradition to which he was referring was that of the murder of Moses. This despite the fact that Sellin himself had given up this suggestion as being completely untenable, even before Freud had written *Moses and Monotheism*. There is no other basis for believing in the existence of more than one Moses, and the fact that Freud believed it is surely one of the clearest examples of wish-fulfilment to be found anywhere.

XI

There is, moreover, the further, apparently insuperable, difficulty that no trace of the teaching of an Egyptian Moses, a follower of Aton, can be found during the Mosaic age. A pure monotheism was only established among the Hebrews hundreds of years later and owed much to the efforts of the prophets. Freud now produced his second hypothesis: the Egyptian

Moses taught the Israelites the monotheistic religion of the great reformer Aton, but after he had been killed all this teaching was repressed and did not emerge until about 500 years later. There is not the slightest proof of this, and the hypothesis was produced because without it Freud could not possibly maintain his main thesis of the relation between an Egyptian and a Hebrew monotheism. It is a fantastic hypothesis, and as Freud returned to it in the last section of his book under the title of "The Return of the Repressed" we shall deal with it later in this chapter.

XII

If the date of the Exodus were known we could judge whether or not there was any possibility of the Ikhnaton period influencing Moses. Unfortunately, the dates of the Exodus and therefore of Moses are not so simply decided as even so profound a scholar as Meek thought they could be. Many of the leading authorities are hopelessly divided on the date of the Exodus. Professor S. A. Cook, Regius Professor of Hebrew in the University of Cambridge, in *The Old Testament. A Re-interpretation* (1936) provides a chronological summary in which he gives the date for Ikhnaton's reign as 1380-1362. The computed date of the Exodus he puts as 1447 B.C. If this were correct, then the age of Moses was considerably before Ikhnaton and there could be no question of the latter influencing the Mosaic age.

Albright, however, gives weighty evidence for placing the Exodus about the year 1290 B.C. and bases this date on the discovery made in 1937 in the remains of the latest Canaanite Lachish of a hieratic inscription dated to the year 1231 B.C. and possibly somewhat later, but in any case not earlier. This proves that the town fell into Israelite hands in or after that year. The Israel stele of Merneptah which is dated 1229 B.C. proved that Israel was already in western Palestine in force but had not yet settled down. If a generation of forty years be allowed for a Wilderness period we arrive at a date not later than about 1260 B.C. for the Exodus. Probably, however, a generation should be allowed for the occupation of eastern Palestine and the advance westwards in force, so this would bring the date to about 1290 B.C. Ikhnaton became Pharaoh in 1377 B.C. and reigned for seventeen years and so to about 1363 or 1360 B.C. If we accept this chronology then it is impossible that Moses could have been influenced directly by Ikhnaton.

In the Summary of Dates given as an appendix by Rowley in his *From Joseph to Joshua* the date of the Exodus is thirty years later than the one given by Albright:

> *circa* 1370 B.C. Joseph taken into Egypt in reign of Ikhnaton, under whom he takes high office.
>
> *circa* 1360 B.C. Descent into Egypt of Hebrews, particularly some of those who had failed to hold Shechem.
>
> *circa* 1300 B.C. Oppression under Rameses II. Hebrews set to build Pithom and Rameses.
>
> *circa* 1290 B.C. Moses born.
>
> *circa* 1260 B.C. Exodus from Egypt under Moses.

Meek in his *Hebrew Origins* places the Exodus much later still: "For the enslaved Hebrews in Egypt a deliverer arose in course of time in the person of Moses, who took advantage of the chaotic state of affairs that developed in Egypt after the death of Seti II (*circa* 1215 B.C.) to lead his people out, or such of them as could or would follow him."[31]

None of these chronologies, all of which are the work of the most distinguished scholars in this field, would make it possible for Moses to be what Freud suggested he was: an adherent of Ikhnaton himself. In themselves, Cook's and also Albright's dates would rule out any possible influence. The other dates for the Exodus are so much after the time of Ikhnaton that, in view of the violent reaction against Ikhnaton and all that he stood for, it is extremely difficult to believe that Moses could have come under his influence.

XIII

If Freud were correct in his main contentions we should expect to find some traces at least of the Aton religion during the Mosaic age. It is right, therefore, to consider the nature of Hebrew religion immediately following the Exodus. What, then, do we find in the Mosaic age? The Israelites believed that Yahweh was their God in a very special sense and, following the leadership of Moses, they believed themselves united with him in a solemn covenant so that they became his 'peculiar people'. They recognized that other nations had their own gods but as far as they were concerned Yahweh alone was to be worshipped. This is not to say that the whole of the nation was always undeviatingly faithful, for at times some of them forsook Yahweh and worshipped the local gods or baalim. But there was always a nucleus who remained faithful to Yahweh.

The anthropomorphic character of Yahweh is very deeply rooted in the Mosaic religion, and in fact he is far more anthropomorphic than the gods we find among the Egyptians or the Mesopotamians. Yahweh is sometimes referred to in a way which suggests that he has a human form although this is usually hidden by his glory. In Exodus XXXIII. 23 Moses is granted the supreme privilege of seeing the back of Yahweh but not the face, because "shall no man see Me and live". He was like his people and so could show love and hatred, joy and sorrow and even revenge and remorse although on a lofty plane. But he stood alone without a consort, or indeed family connections of any kind. In all this we are in a different atmosphere from the surrounding forms of religion. For instance the sun had no significant part to play at all. Yahweh is an anthropomorphic Supreme Being and not a solar or nature deity like Murduk, Amon-Re or Aton. Aton could be represented by a solar disc from which human hands emanated, whereas there was no physical representation of Yahweh whatsoever. There was nothing remote about him for he was interested in everything his people did, and Israel recognized Yahweh less and less as a Supreme Being or High

God and more as a God who was first interested in them as individuals and as a nation, and so in their history, and finally in the history of the whole world.

Yahweh was not restricted to any special place. He was lord of all the cosmic forces and controlled the sun, the moon and the storm, but at the same time he was not identified with any of them. He dwelt in Heaven but could come down to a lofty mountain like Sinai, or to a shrine like the Tabernacle or to any place he might choose.

The tradition representing Moses as a lawgiver is so strong that probably the basis at least of such a statement as the Ten Commandments does go back to the movement associated with his name. It is unlikely to be earlier, and if with Meek and other Semitic scholars we accept them as being at least in general agreement with the movement which bears the name of Moses, we can see the force of the point which Meek makes in referring to the first commandment: "However the most we can claim for Moses in it is monolatry".[32]

XIV

During the middle of the eighth century B.C. there arose a group of men, the prophets, who purified the traditional religion and taught a conception of God which was undoubtedly pure monotheism and of a remarkable kind. Not only was God one but he was perfectly good and he demanded goodness from his followers. The teaching about Yahweh during this age is summed up by T. H. Robinson in *The Teachers' Commentary*.*

(*a*) Yahweh is Law. He was no capricious being like the gods of most nations but was consistent in all His actions.

(*b*) Yahweh is Lord of Nature. He was God of Creation and there was no other God responsible for any part of nature.

(*c*) Yahweh is Lord of History. He was no longer a tribal God but controlled the whole political world.

* 14th edition, 1946.

(*d*) Yahweh is the Lord of the end of things. At the end of all things Yahweh would vindicate, not Israel against other nations, but the principles of righteousness against Israel as His character required.

(*e*) Yahweh is Lord of Universal Morality. His interest in human conduct did not spring merely from the pride of a god who had laid down certain commands on a particular people but He watched over the actions of men everywhere and His Laws were valid for all nations whether they knew it or not for they were based on the nature of personality.

(*f*) Yahweh makes no ritual demands. It is righteousness He asks, not sacrifice, and it is hopeless to offer the latter as a substitute for the former.

(*g*) Yahweh is, in a special sense, the God of Israel. Although He is the Lord of the whole world, yet He has chosen Israel for His own purposes. She has then special privileges but also special responsibilities and if she fails to meet them she will receive special punishment.

This is monotheism but it is not the religion of Aton. Freud believed that it was nothing more than the emergence of the repressed from the racial unconscious. Yet surely the great prophets had something vital to do in the formulation of this unique conception of God. It was influenced by the past history of Israel and expressed the spirit of that nation. The prophets were great individualists and each emphasized the particular aspect of the general teaching which appealed most strongly to him. Hosea, speaking from the deep experiences of his own married life, spoke of love. Amos insisted on justice, on fair dealing between man and man. Isaiah's message was concerned with holiness and the importance of complete consecration on the part of Israel to Yahweh in recognition of the consecration and holiness of Yahweh towards Israel. The message is the expression of the prophet, and the prophet, although influenced by the nation, was an individual with his own particular utterance. As he himself recognized, he was responsible for the message he had to proclaim and was no mere sounding-board delivering a strange teaching from the depths of a racial unconscious which, all unknown to him, came through a first unknown Moses, from the reformer Ikhnaton.

The authors of *Before Philosophy* came to the definite conclusion that the religious thought of the Hebrews belonged to an entirely different atmosphere from that of Egypt and Mesopotamia. This book is of importance because in it a group of competent scholars survey the whole background with which *Moses and Monotheism* deals. In a final chapter on "The Emancipation of Thought from Myth" Professor and Mrs. Frankfort insist on the overwhelming distinction between Egyptian and Mesopotamian thought and belief and that of the Hebrews, and use as an illustration the Hebrew teaching about Yahweh:

> The Hebrews arrived late upon the scene and settled in a country pervaded by influences from the two superior adjacent cultures. One would expect the newcomers to have assimilated alien modes of thought, since these were supported by such vast prestige. Untold immigrants from deserts and mountains had done so in the past; and many individual Hebrews did, in fact, conform to the ways of the Gentiles. But assimilation was not characteristic for Hebrew thought. On the contrary, it held out with a peculiar stubbornness and insolence against the wisdom of Israel's neighbours. It is possible to detect the reflection of Egyptian and Mesopotamian beliefs in many episodes of the Old Testament; but the overwhelming impression left by that document is one, not of derivation, but of originality.[33]

Meek came to a similar conclusion: "It is one of the enigmas of history that the Hebrews were so little affected by the religion of Egypt, when both history and archaeology show such intimate contacts between the two."[34]

I

XV

Man is seldom a complete innovator in anything important and usually less so in religion than elsewhere. If Egypt was not the spiritual home of the religion of the Mosaic age where is that to be found?

One of the most interesting views, which admittedly is not shared by all scholars, is that the name of Yahweh and certain features of the Mosaic teaching about religion were derived from the Kenites, who were a nomadic tribe of the south of Palestine closely associated with the Amalekites. This view is supported and discussed in Rowley's Schweich Lectures *From Joseph to Joshua.**

The Biblical record describes how Moses had to leave Egypt for fear that his murder of an Egyptian would be discovered. We know that he went down to Midian and there married a daughter of Jethro. Rowley advances the interesting suggestion that a Levite belonging to the Israelite group that went down into Egypt could have married a Kenite woman. The mother of Moses had a name which was compounded with the name Yahweh, and even if we judged by that alone it would look as if an ancestor of Moses on his mother's side had married a Kenite woman. This at any rate would explain why, when Moses fled from Egypt, he went to a Kenite settlement; he could have gone there because they were his mother's people, just as Jacob, when he fled from Esau, went to his mother's kindred. During the period that Moses spent in the household of Jethro he would have come into touch with the religion professed by the priest Jethro. Possibly during that time Moses experienced a deep religious conversion, and became convinced that this God about whom he had now learnt so much was the powerful God who would deliver his fellow-countrymen from their bondage in Egypt. So he returned to that country and led his people out, to the sacred mountain of Sinai. Those, therefore, whom he led would have a different background from his own—if we can

* Oxford University Press (1950).

rely on these conjectures—and so, according to their traditions, the worship of Yahweh began with the coming of Moses to deliver them and the acceptance of the solemn Covenant of Sinai. This theory would at any rate help to explain the religion of the Mosaic age without straining our credulity to the extent that Freud does.

As we know, the father-in-law of Moses is sometimes called Jethro, a priest of Midian, and sometimes Reuel, a priest of Midian. Elsewhere it is stated that Hohab, the son of Reuel, was a Kenite and thus it would appear that the father-in-law of Moses was a Kenite. We also know that when Moses led the Israelites out of Egypt he was met by his father-in-law who, after he had heard of the great deliverance wrought by Yahweh, cried: "Now I know that Yahweh is greater than all the gods" (Exod. xviii. 11). He it was who then offered sacrifice to God and, after he had given Moses advice, left. The sacrifice at which Jethro officiated for the elders of Israel must have been the sacrifice to the God Yahweh, and it is probable that this Yahweh was the God to whom Jethro was priest. We can only understand his joy at the evidence of Yahweh's great power if Yahweh were the God whom he already served.

XVI

There is a case for believing that monotheistic tendencies are present in all forms of religion which have a place for gods.* In the widespread beliefs in the All-Father, High Gods and Supreme Deities there exists material which may contain the seed of all later forms of monotheism. What is extremely probable is that even among primitive people there have been stronger monotheistic tendencies than have usually been acknowledged. Among all such people at certain stages there have been reflective minds aware that the existence of one God is a possibility. Such tendencies may be numbered among the influences in the background from which the Yahweh religion developed.

* See E. O. James, *The Beginnings of Religion*, and N. Micklam, *Religion* (Home University Library).

The Yahweh of the Mosaic age is certainly more in accord with this atmosphere than with the speculative religion of the school of Ikhnaton.

XVII

Repression is defined in a glossary at the end of *Moses and Monotheism* as "the keeping of unacceptable ideas from consciousness, i.e. in the 'unconscious'". This process Freud found repeatedly in his analytical work, but in *Moses and Monotheism* he claimed that just as the individual represses so does the race or mass: "The masses, too, retain an impression of the past in unconscious memory traces".[35] Further passages make clear exactly what Freud is claiming for the part of repression in the racial unconscious. "The murder of the Father was brought home to the Jews, for fate decreed that they should repeat it on the person of Moses, an eminent father substitute."[36] "The murder of Moses was such a repetition, and later on the supposed judicial murder of Christ, so that these events move into the foreground as causative agents."[37] Freud even goes so far as to include the ideas of former ages among the contents of the racial unconscious: " . . . the archaic heritage of mankind includes not only dispositions, but also ideational contents, memory-traces of the experiences of former generations."[38]

What has been repressed in the racial unconscious can, so Freud claimed, return in the same way as it does with the individual neurosis, and he illustrated his theme by the material given in *Moses and Monotheism*.

We can classify what Freud treated as the return of the repressed in the following way:

1. The memory of the Great Crime—the killing of the primaeval father.
2. The primaeval experience in the human family where in the return of the repressed the figure of the father, grown still more gigantic than even early experience in childhood made him, is given the status of a deity.

3. Such ideational material as the teaching by an Egyptian
   Moses of the monotheism which he had derived from
   Ikhnaton.

Freud repeated in *Moses and Monotheism* the theme of the
slaying of the primal father of the horde and his belief that the
knowledge of this crime remains in the racial unconscious and
creates a continuing sense of guilt: ". . . I have no qualms in saying that men have always known—in this particular way—that
once upon a time they had a primaeval father and killed him".[39]
The memory and the guilt were always there, ready to return
just like an outbreak of neurosis in the individual. Freud seized
the briefly-held hypothesis of Sellin that the Israelites had killed
the father of their race, Moses, and this murder he maintained
was a repetition of the killing of the primal father. It made the
Great Crime real to the race, and while remaining deeply buried
in the racial unconscious increased the sense of guilt which continued to haunt the Israelites.

He applied what he believed to be the implications of this
to the Christian religion. The doctrine of original sin became
prominent in the early Church, but the significance of this for
him was that it symbolized in the unconscious the murder of
the primaeval father. Saul might say "It is because we killed God
the Father that we are so unhappy",[40] but the true source of the
guilt and so of the unhappiness was the primaeval murder.
Salvation from this original sin was to be found through a
sacrificial death, and so Christianity was to be interpreted in
the following way: "Its main doctrine, to be sure, was the
reconciliation with God the Father, the expiation of the crime
committed against Him; but the other side of the relationship
manifested itself in the Son—who had taken the guilt on his
shoulders—becoming God himself beside the Father and in
truth in place of the Father. Originally a Father religion, Christianity became a Son religion. The fate of having to displace the
Father it could not escape."[41] The true significance of Christianity was, Freud claimed, that it combined a return of the

repressed in this particular sense and a way of dealing with it.

Freud also believed that Moses, in teaching his followers about the one God, was not giving them a new idea "for it meant the re-animation of primaeval experience in the human family that had long ago faded from the conscious memory of mankind".[42] He believed that the Father loomed as a gigantic figure in primaeval times and, raised to the status of a deity in the racial unconscious, returned to the memory of mankind.

XVIII

This view of the powers of the racial unconscious is a highly original one, and so much is built on it that it merits careful examination. Ordinarily we think of repression as being a very individual affair and we do not expect what has been repressed in one person to emerge from someone else. It is surprising to claim that ideational contents are carried in a racial unconscious for hundreds of years. And as Freud admits: "This state of affairs is made more difficult, it is true, by the present attitude of biological science which rejects the idea of acquired qualities being transmitted to descendants. I admit, in all modesty, that in spite of this I cannot picture biological development proceeding without taking this factor into account."[43] There is admittedly a process of repression relating to individuals and possibly a collective unconscious which preserves, as Jung maintains, important racial experiences which are stamped in over endless years and function in a form similar to what we mean by instincts. But nothing is known of any process which would preserve the speculative ideas of Ikhnaton on monotheism and religion through Moses in the unconscious of another nation for hundreds of years. It is surely more credible to believe that the thought and experience of such prophets as Amos, Hosea, Isaiah and Jeremiah played some part, and that not a minor one, in the establishment of ethical monotheism among the Hebrews. If Ikhnaton had his vision, that is no reason why the great eighth-century prophets should not have had theirs.

Freud's argument that monotheistic teaching was latent for hundreds of years was a dangerous one for him to use, especially when he went on to claim that Ikhnaton was the first monotheist in history. According to his contention about the nature of the unconscious, we have no right to assume this, for monotheism might have remained latent in the unconscious of the Egyptian nation for hundreds of years to emerge during the Eighteenth Dynasty. There might have been monotheistic teaching among the Hyksos who invaded Egypt long before Ikhnaton and if, as some maintain, the Hyksos were Semites, all kinds of interesting possibilities would arise. Moreover those who, like Schmidt, argue for a universal primitive monotheism could explain by means of this theory how it had been repressed at various periods. Freud's hypothesis could be used in many directions if it could be accepted, but it cannot, and all the vast structure which he built on it was falsely based: consequently most of his arguments about the nature and contents of religious belief put forward in *Moses and Monotheism* and also in some of his other works have no weight. That, we believe, is the correct conclusion.

There are two aspects to Freud's theories about the rôle of Moses in the racial unconscious. One is that he is a father imago: "Without doubt it must have been a tremendous father imago that stooped in the person of Moses to tell the poor Jewish labourers that they were his dear children."[44] Moses reanimated the primaeval experience in the human family and as a father imago helped to raise this to the status of deity. His other rôle was to pass on the teachings of Ikhnaton which then remained latent for so long, together with memories of the slaying of Moses.

There is, however, one flaw in Freud's argument that Moses reanimated the experience of the primaeval family situation and the slaying of the primal father. He stated that the first Moses was not the Father of Israel, but an idealistic Egyptian who determined to continue the Aton religion through the foreign Israelites. His motives were propagandist and so he was not a good substitute for the primal father. But the whole point of the argument in

Totem and Taboo, repeated in *Moses and Monotheism*, was that the father of the horde was killed not because he was an aggressive and dominating figure, but through sexual jealousy: "All females were his property, the wives and daughters in his own horde as well as perhaps also those robbed from other hordes. The fate of the sons was a hard one; if they excited the father's jealousy they were killed or castrated or driven out."[45] After they revolted and killed him they realized the futility of killing each other to obtain the succession which they desired, so "Each renounced the ideal of gaining for himself the position of father, of possessing his mother or sister. With this the taboo of incest and the law of exogamy came into being."[46] There is not the slightest reason anywhere to think that anyone could even have wished to murder Moses through motives of this kind.

If God is nothing but 'an exalted father', a projection from the primaeval family situation, and Moses merely another example of him and a return of this repressed material, what is the point of the elaborate theory that it was Ikhnaton who first produced the speculation of monotheism, which then spread through an Egyptian Moses, remaining latent in the racial unconscious until it was made active once more in the eighth century? Freud was trying to explain the emergence of monotheism through his concept of the racial unconscious in two ways, one through an experience of the primaeval family, common to the whole human race, and the other through the retaining by the racial unconscious of the ideational contents transmitted through Moses. If the former were operative, monotheism would arise everywhere. The latter would be unnecessary and surely could not be separately recognized.

XIX

What Freud had to say about the place of Jesus Christ and Paul does not fit well into the structure of *Moses and Monotheism*, although he tried to make it do so. According to Freud Moses came from Egypt with his new teaching, and was killed, later becoming a tremendous father imago. Approximately 1,300 or

1,400 years after his death a Jew was killed, a son of the nation, to atone for the deed of his brothers in killing Moses, and through him repeating the Great Crime. In actual fact He did not save His brothers from their guilt for most of them did not accept Him as their Saviour. He was accepted as Saviour by the Gentiles, although there could be no question of their racial unconscious being burdened with the guilt of killing Moses.

All this may appear to fit in perfectly with the requirements of psychoanalytical reasoning. Yet it might appear to those who are accustomed to use other modes of reasoning as well, that it had been made to fit in too neatly. Since the time when Freud put forward the obscure hypothesis of the slaying of the primal father, ethnologists have described it as nonsense. Freud knew this, and even admitted it in *Moses and Monotheism*, but answered that he preferred to hold on to his own version. Facts of history, sound anthropology, convincing psychology in relation to the racial unconscious, evidence worthy of serious consideration or even solid argument—none of these is prominent in *Moses and Monotheism*.

NOTES TO CHAPTER 5

[1] S. Freud, *Moses and Monotheism*, trans. K. Jones. London, Hogarth Press (1939), p. 79.

[2] W. F. Albright, *From the Stone Age to Christianity*. Baltimore, The Johns Hopkins Press (1946), pp. 74-5.

[3] Helen Walker Puner, *Freud*. London, Grey Walls Press (1949), p. 252.

[4] J. H. Breasted, *The Dawn of Conscience*. London, Charles Scribner's Sons, (1934), p. 350 (quoted in *Moses and Monotheism*, p. 13).

[5] S. Freud, *op. cit.*, pp. 22-3.

[6] *Ibid.*, p. 23.

[7] *Ibid.*, pp. 62-3.

[8] W. F. Albright, *op. cit.*, p. 43.

[9] S. Freud, *op. cit.*, p. 46.

[10] *Ibid.*, p. 44.

[11] *Ibid.*, pp. 53-4.

[12] Exod. vi. 10-13.

[13] Exod. vii. 1-2.

[14] J. D. S. Pendlebury, *Tell el-Amarna*. London, Lovat Dickson & Thompson (1935), pp. 159-60.

[15] *Ibid.*, p. 15.

[16] H. & H. A. Frankfort, John A. Wilson and T. Jacobsen, *Before Philosophy*. London, Pelican Books (1949), p. 98.

[17] *Ibid.*, p. 58.

[18] *Ibid.*, p. 75.

[19] *Ibid.*, p. 75.

[20] *Ibid.*, pp. 75-6.

[21] T. J. Meek, *Hebrew Origins*. New York, Harper (1950), p. 206.

[22] S. Freud, *op. cit.*, p. 51.

[23] *Ibid.*, p. 55.

[24] *Ibid.*, pp. 55-6.

[25] *Ibid.*, p. 56.

[26] *Ibid.*, p. 58.

[27] *Ibid.*, p. 60.

[28] *Ibid.*, p. 60.

[29] *Ibid.*, p. 98.

[30] *Ibid.*, pp. 59-60.

[31] T. J. Meek, *op. cit.*, p. 38.

[32] *Ibid.*, p. 208.

[33] H. & H. A. Frankfort, John A. Wilson and T. Jacobsen, *op. cit.*, p. 241.

[34] T. J. Meek, *op. cit.*, p. 207.

[35] S. Freud, *op. cit.*, p. 151.

[36] *Ibid.*, p. 143.

[37] *Ibid.*, p. 162.

[38] *Ibid.*, p. 159.

[39] *Ibid.*, p. 161.

[40] *Ibid.*, p. 213.

[41] *Ibid.*, pp. 214-15.

[42] *Ibid.*, p. 204.

[43] *Ibid.*, p. 160.

[44] *Ibid.*, p. 174.

[45] *Ibid.*, pp. 130-1.

[46] *Ibid.*, p. 132.

6

The Limits of Psychoanalysis

"Freud's flashing originality as a psychologist was balanced by
an uncritical mediocrity as a philosopher: he took over the atomic
materialism of the scientific philosophy current in his youth and,
apart from his biological inheritance, he regarded the individual
as a self-contained unit, upon whose assertive will society acted
as a check, a curb, a censor."

LEWIS MUMFORD, *The Condition of Man* (p. 363).

"L'incrédulité est un croyance, une religion très exigeante."

ALPHONSE KARR.

I

ALTHOUGH Freud wrote extensively on religion these
writings now appear to be largely irrelevant. It might be
argued that this is because he began writing on this subject nearly
fifty years ago. Against this contention must be set the fact that
the material in such books as his *Introductory Lectures on Psychoanalysis*, *The Interpretation of Dreams*, and indeed on psychology
in general, although written long ago, is still convincing and
remains a contribution of importance. The modifications which
one would think necessary are not more than one might expect
time and further work to bring. There can be no doubt that we
are dealing with pioneer work of lasting significance. In these
works Freud was dealing with material on which he was qualified
to write and, more than this, the brilliance which he possessed,
amounting to genius, found its scope in this realm. When he
dealt with anthropology, history and religion he was an amateur,
and one moreover with no time to undertake the research
which would act as a safeguard against rash and unfounded
judgments.

Freud, as we have seen, was fifty-one before he wrote on the subject of religion at all and even then his first contribution amounted to a few pages only. It is impossible to know exactly why he did not write on this subject until the later years of his life. One reason might well be that since he originally thought that religion, as one of man's infantile illusions, had no future, it could be left to its own demise. For an illusion, however, it appeared to be remarkably healthy and persistent and, as time went on, Freud attempted to reveal the psychological processes which sustained it.

Another reason may have been that he was curbed in these early years by scientific caution. The spirit of the Freud who had carried out research on the spinal cord of the *Ammocoetes Petromyzon* and later had concentrated on the medulla oblongata was still on guard, but as the years went by he was no longer that kind of scientist, and in fact he achieved his most valuable work just because he was not. The safeguards and controls of scientific method were cast off too freely in some directions and he was apt to speculate rashly, particularly in his contributions to religious psychology.

It is obvious that he became increasingly critical of religious belief. In *Totem and Taboo* he qualified some of his more radical conclusions, and in places is cautious in his approach. In writing of the influence of the father on the concept of God he admitted that, although the father has an obvious influence, this is quite apart from "all the other origins and meanings of god upon which psychoanalysis can throw no light".[1] He also stated in the same work that psychoanalysis would not be tempted to derive anything so complicated as religion from a single source. To assess the relative importance of the mechanism discussed in *Totem and Taboo* to the beginnings of religion would require a synthesis from many fields of research, a course which Freud admits would exceed both the means and intentions of the psychoanalyst.[2]

Fifteen years later he wrote *The Future of an Illusion*, and in this he claimed that he could explain the origins of religious ideas: "I have tried to show that religious ideas have sprung from the same need as all the other achievements of culture: from the necessity for defending itself against the crushing supremacy of nature."[3]

In his essay "A Philosophy of Life" first published in 1933, he was even more definite. He maintained that in relation to the external world man is still a child and cannot give up the protections he enjoyed as a child. Man's belief in God has a twofold origin: the emotional strength of the memory image of the father exalted into a deity, and his lasting need for protection.[4]

Near the end of *Moses and Monotheism* he felt it necessary to give one of the reasons why he could not accept a religious interpretation of life, although he confessed that he would like to do so. He was convinced that "the religious argument is based on an optimistic and idealistic premise".[5] He did not weigh the consideration that he might be unable to accept such a solution partly at least because of his own profoundly pessimistic nature. Here in his last book all caution had gone, and he proclaimed both his atheism once again and his conviction that religious belief could be explained psychologically: "I do not believe that one supreme great God 'exists' to-day, but I believe that in primaeval times there was one person who must needs appear gigantic and who, raised to the status of a deity, returned to the memory of men".[6]

II

Psychoanalysis proclaims the supreme influence of the early years in life. It is a reductive system of analysis. Neurotic traits, character qualities and personal beliefs are, it assumes, determined by our earliest experiences. Freud emphasized this approach in his analytical works and expounded it in his writings with the utmost thoroughness. He failed, however, to allow for this influence in his own life for he did not appear to realize the extent to which his own views about religion were determined by his upbringing. Yet from what we know of his early days, of the predominant scientific outlook of that period, and of the nature of his medical training, we might with certainty deduce his proneness to accept the views he did.

In Chapter I we have described the Jewish home into which he was born where the old religious customs and practices were falling into disuse and religion itself no longer appeared to be a force. In fact there is some evidence that his father became a free-thinker. Certainly there is evidence that Freud himself was an atheist from the early years of his life. Moreover, as a Jew, he was a member of an unpopular minority and it would be more than strange if he had not resented this unpopularity. His resentment would naturally be against the persecutors of his race, namely the Christian majority. Certainly Freud would not be favourably disposed towards that which gave the Christians their name—the Christian Faith. In *Totem and Taboo* we are given a version of its dark origins; it arose from the anarchy and murder in the primal horde and never succeeded in being more than a sublimation of those dark forces.

The attitude towards the Christian community in the Jewish circle of which Freud was a member is shown by what happened when one of Martha's uncles, Michael Bernays, renounced the Jewish faith because, it was said, he desired professional advancement not possible to a Jew, and became Professor of German at the University of Munich. His brother Jakob, who taught Latin and Greek at the University of Heidelberg, followed the Jewish custom of going into mourning because of this apostasy.

Freud was a loyal member of the Jewish race although he did not share its religious beliefs. His aggression must have been aroused against those who were guilty of anti-Semitism, and the influence of this must be allowed for when reading his comments upon the religious faith of the Christians, especially as he himself was convinced that all religion was an illusion.

III

He accepted uncritically the predominant scientific outlook of his age as a complete revelation of truth. But he nowhere defines science, and spelling it with a capital letter as he sometimes did was no substitute for a careful definition and an examination of its nature. It is possible to maintain either that science can only give a partial interpretation of the truth, or to claim that no truth is knowable apart from a scientific approach. In biological circles towards the end of the nineteenth century the latter claim was made and Haeckel was one of its chief exponents. It was this type of *scientism* which Freud adopted. In it there was no place for philosophy or religion. Science was all. But he never proved, or attempted to prove, that science contains the sum total of knowledge and is the sole path to reality. His genius was not that of a scientist unless that term is interpreted in a very different way from that understood during the nineteenth century. He arrived at insights rather than findings, and speculation was more in evidence than research. But 'insight', 'intuition' and 'speculation' were suspect in the scientific milieu of his day, and possibly this is why he so loudly proclaimed his adherence to science and its glorious possibilities. He believed that unless his work was regarded as scientific it would be undervalued. While consciously clinging to orthodox science, his own methods and theories did not accord well with its spirit. If he did not realize this his old teachers, such as Brücke and Meynert, did. Even in his later and clearly speculative writings he continued to preach the virtues of science and, in particular, the scientific method and the hopes that it gave to mankind. Science became Freud's faith and psychoanalysis his sect. Whatever illusions other men might or might not possess, his illusion was science. As H. W. Puner writes in her *Freud:* "Thus, one of the world's most determined disillusionists falls into the trap of ruthlessly tearing from his life one of man's great 'illusions', only to substitute for it another."[7]

IV

Freud was strengthened in his conviction that religion was an illusion because of what he believed about the unconscious. Thus his views of the nature and scope of the unconscious must be briefly examined. There were thinkers long before him who assumed that unconscious processes took place in the mind. Plato even anticipated the function of wish-fulfilment in dreams which is now a commonplace of psychoanalytical theory. Leibnitz gave an important place to unconscious cognitive processes. Schopenhauer, Herbert, Hartmann each made significant contributions in preparing the way for more satisfactory views on the subject, for each in some form or other allowed a place for it. It is also clear now that the work of Bernheim, Charcot, Janet, Boudouin and many others anticipated the theories produced by Freud, of the dynamic nature of the unconscious. Evidence derived from the study of motor automatisms, multiple personality, the phenomena of suggestion and hypnotism, was almost conclusive regarding the existence of mental activity not consciously known.

The spirit of the age prepared the way for Freud, but his genius was such that he saw the significance of the unconscious in a new way. Yet, apart from what had gone before, he probably would not have formed his theories, and possibly if he had not gone to Paris and studied under Charcot, and also witnessed the work of Bernheim at Nancy, he might have remained merely a highly competent neurologist. There was, however, genius of a high order in Freud's achievement, for with those who had gone before, even Hartmann, the unconscious was either thought of as some addition to consciousness, or as being general in its nature. It was not for them, as it was for Freud, the definite reality capable of being explored by the methods of free association and dream analysis. Freud's greatest discovery was to take the dynamic unconscious as the most powerful motive force in the mind. Also he believed that it could be fully explored. Perhaps he was too self-assured about his ability to plumb its depths and chart its dimensions. Possibly he over-simplified the nature of the work which had to be done and perhaps this gave him the advantage of setting out on his quest with great self-confidence.

The instruments of the earliest explorer are apt to be crude in most realms, and the findings match the tools. Although Freud gradually modified his theories he failed to realize the complexity of the material with which he was dealing, and although he was undoubtedly correct in his general insistence on the dynamic nature of the unconscious, he was probably too narrow in his interpretation of its contents. It is difficult to achieve sufficient objectivity to make valid pronouncements about the fundamental nature of the mind. The individual observer must allow for his own limitations in knowledge, temperament, character and the bias of his own social patterns or culture. Freud was the heir of Darwin, Helmholtz and Brücke and he judged universal man in an individualistic setting, by evidence produced almost wholly by his Viennese patients. In his age the conspiracy of silence about sex applied to continental medical circles as well as to society in general. It is well known that Freud's early observations on the place of sex and the necessity for making enquiries about the sexual life of patients were received with disapproval by his medical colleagues. Yet he saw that the place of sexuality in normal life was not clearly recognized, and that sexual maladjustment was an important factor in the causation of many neuroses. Therefore it is not surprising that in his particular society Freud found little but sexuality in the unconscious, for we know that this is exactly what was repressed at that time.

As time went on Freud himself, as was to be expected, widened his conception of the unconscious. He came to see the place which aggression occupied in it. There was even the addition of the death instinct. Mental life was pictured in terms of the id, the ego and the super-ego. He was influenced by Jung's theories about the collective unconscious, and acknowledged this indebtedness both in *Totem and Taboo*[8] and in *An Autobiographical Study*.[9] Yet he was narrow and dogmatic in his views about the nature of the unconscious and also about symbolism. This was surely one reason why such colleagues as Jung and Adler felt that they had to leave the psychoanalytical fold. We have the impression that Freud discovered a bay but thought that he had charted the oceans. The unconscious is not easily mapped, nor can the

K

contents of the conscious, such as art and religion, be so simply and convincingly explained as he imagined. The territory of the unconscious is both vaster and more complex than he realized. For this reason his attempted explanations of religious experience in terms of the unconscious processes familiar to him are far too simple, as indeed are his views of the nature of the unconscious itself. The sources and phenomena of religious experience and belief are more profound than Freud believed.

V

Firm in his conviction that religious belief must be based on an illusion, he concerned himself with attempts to discover its causes. One of the first principles of psychoanalysis was the emphasis it placed on causation. Freud, in seeking the cause of the illusion, proceeded as he would have done in studying an individual's neurosis, and he had no doubts about the value of this procedure, for to him religion was a mass neurosis. In *Totem and Taboo* he dealt at length with the causes of religion, and our discussion of that book has shown how difficult it is to be sure that the cause or causes of complicated behaviour or conscious beliefs have all been found.

As a determinist he thought that causes were all-important. This is to be doubted for there is the possibility at least that purpose may play a large part in the structure of our mental life, in neurosis, and in religious beliefs. At this point there is a great difference between the approach of Freud and that of Jung to the contents of the unconscious. Freud sought for the ultimate causes of behaviour and the repressions of the contents of the conscious, whereas Jung not only allows for these influences but also for the possibility of others. He considers the propensity of the mind to compensate in one direction or the other, to produce purposively a conflict of opposites and for the individual unconsciously, but nevertheless purposively, to seek integration. There is sufficient in this approach, as well as in others, to throw doubt on the validity of Freud's exclusive concern with causation, and even if causes were the sole factors involved, religious phenomena are so complicated that it is doubtful if any one cause or even a list of causes could be produced to provide a completely satisfactory explanation.

VI

Closely allied with his efforts to explain religion by revealing its causes was his attempt to discover the motives which produced and sustained it. The reply to this is in part similar to what has been said above concerning Freud's emphasis on causation. We may discover a number of motives but they may not be the most important ones. We can trace several motives for Freud's atheism but these do not have the slightest relevance as to whether or not atheism is the truth. The issue of validity is entirely different from that of motivation and must be approached in a different way. In religion this will certainly involve theological, philosophical and historical considerations at least. Without admitting this, Freud unconsciously recognized it, for he philosophized about science and religion but without realizing what he was doing and without the necessary equipment or natural aptitude in these realms. Fundamentally, however, he believed that the motives producing and sustaining religion could be revealed, and that when they were, religious phenomena could be shown to possess psychological origins. But however far a study of the motives involved may be taken, and however convincing the results may be, the issue of validity clearly belongs to an entirely different realm.

VII

Another serious shortcoming in Freud's treatment of religion was his tendency to speculate and generalize far too readily and to fit everything into his requirements, his preconceived system. Examples of this abound in his writings on religious psychology and have been given in previous chapters.

The underlying reason for this was that he believed that he had an unlimited mandate to speculate on this and other subjects, and he revealed why in *Moses and Monotheism*. Near the beginning of that book he wrote: "the considerations thus reached [in this book] will impress only that minority of readers familiar with analytical reasoning and able to appreciate its conclusions."[10] The adoption of such a standpoint, psychoanalytical totalitarianism, forestalls all criticisms, for only those unfamiliar with analytical reasoning would dare to make them, and anything they might say could safely be disregarded on the grounds that they were not able to appreciate its conclusions. This was the attitude, the conviction to which Freud came, and so he made himself and those who rigorously followed him unassailable, impervious to criticism. However wild and ill-founded were the conclusions to which he came, as for example those in *Moses and Monotheism*, his answer was that they fitted into the requirements of psychoanalytical reasoning. This approach, which we have called psychoanalytical totalitarianism, was not by any means confined to religion, for anthropology could be treated in this way as it was in *Totem and Taboo*. His anthropological theories came in for severe criticism, but twenty-five years later he showed what he thought of the experts on this subject for he wrote in *Moses and Monotheism* that although ethnologists had "without exception discarded Robertson Smith's theories",[11] he himself was going to continue to use them because they served his analytical work.

Freud called this 'analytical reasoning'! Logicians would call it begging the question. Those who had learnt some of the lessons which can profitably be learnt from psychoanalysis would call it the process of rationalization. We can all see that it led to rash generalizations and more than doubtful conclusions. And in no realm did Freud apply this approach more vigorously than in dealing with religion.

VIII

Nevertheless, by whatever means he sought to establish them, it must be admitted that some of his statements were true. Wish-fulfilment *can* play a part in the form which religious belief takes, as can projection and rationalization. Some of the motives involved in a person's religion *may* be made known through psychoanalysis. His mistake was to believe that *everything* could be known and understood. Yet whatever other element may be present Herbert Spencer was surely right when he wrote: "To the aboriginal man and to every civilized child the problem of the Universe suggests itself. What is it? and whence comes it? are questions that press for a solution, when from time to time, the imagination rises above daily trivialities."[12] There is nothing pathological about this quest and that it occurs is a fact, easily and frequently observed, and it provides no evidence for the existence of a mass neurosis, for it merely means that man has the power to reason and naturally asks questions. Freud refused to recognize the importance of questions to which his version of science could give no answer. This searching for an answer to the all-important questions for man is, however, one of the sources of religion and a part of man's normal experience. Freud either ignored this tendency or treated it as abnormal.

As we have repeatedly said, Freud was a man of integrity possessing an adventurous mind. In spite of this he ended by living in an extremely narrow world because of the assumptions he made, namely that religion was false; that science was of transcendent importance; and that in psychoanalysis lay a key to the complete understanding of man. He believed that this was the totality of existence. But because Freud limited his range of vision there is no proof, as he assumed, that he had seen everything.

Freud attempted to understand religious phenomena but never as something to be taken seriously. His assumption was that religion was an illusion, and understanding for him in the end came to mean explaining it. Lewis Mumford puts the matter bluntly in *The Condition of Man*: "One who had disclosed the significance of even 'accidental' behaviour in everyday life should not have been so ready to treat religion as a gigantic vermiform appendix: a meaningless vestigial organ that might poison the personality but had never had a positive function."[13]

NOTES TO CHAPTER 6

[1] S. Freud, *Totem and Taboo*, trans. A. A. Brill. London, Pelican Books edn. (1938), p. 196.

[2] *Ibid.*, p. 138.

[3] S. Freud, *The Future of an Illusion*, trans. W. D. Robson-Scott. London, Hogarth Press (1928), pp. 36-7.

[4] S. Freud, *New Introductory Lectures on Psycho-Analysis*, trans. W. J. H. Sprott (2nd edn.). London, Hogarth Press (1937), p. 209.

[5] S. Freud, *Moses and Monotheism*, trans. K. Jones. London, Hogarth Press 1939), p. 203.

[6] *Ibid.*, p. 204.

[7] Helen Walker Puner, *Freud*. London, Grey Walls Press (1949), p. 220.

[8] S. Freud, *Totem and Taboo*, p. 5.

[9] S. Freud, *An Autobiographical Study*, trans. James Strachey. London, Hogarth Press (1935), p. 121.

[10] S. Freud, *Moses and Monotheism*, p. 15.

[11] *Ibid.*, p. 207.

[12] H. Spencer, *First Principles* (1st edn.). London, Harrison & Sons (1863).

[13] L. Mumford, *The Condition of Man*. London, Martin Secker & Warburg (1944), p. 364.

Index

WARREN, H. C., 81
Wilson, John A., 105, 106
Wish-fulfilment, 15, 74, 76-8, 80, 81, 86,
    90, 109, 130, 134
Wishful thinking, 76-9, 81, 84
Wittels, F., 8-9

YAHWEH, religion of, 108, 112-18
Young, Edward, 80

ZIPPORAH, 101

Daddy. Christmas 1956
from Vernon.